To

_____

From

_____

Date

_____

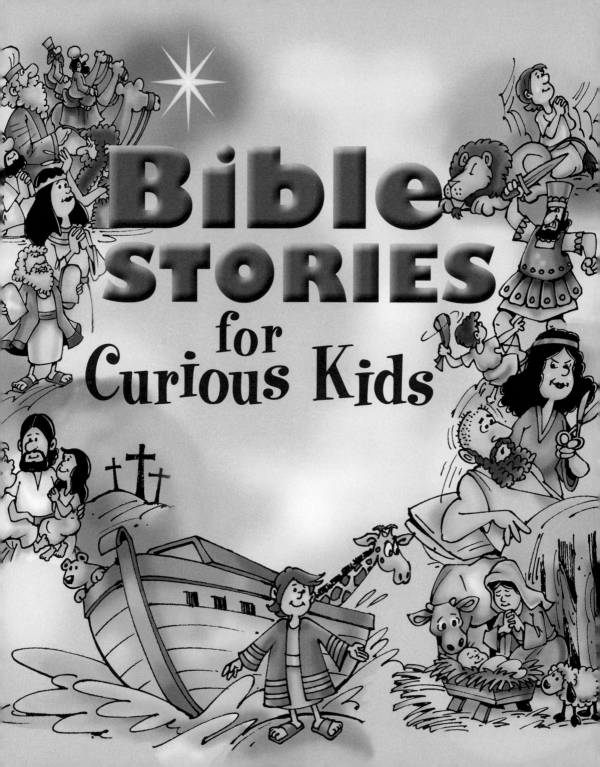

Bible STORIES
for Curious Kids

Published by Standard Publishing, Cincinnati, Ohio

www.standardpub.com

Copyright © 2010 by Educational Publishing Concepts, Wheaton, IL 60189

Printed in: SE Asia

Project editor: Elaina Meyers

Cover design: Diane Bay and Sandra Wimmer

Illustrations by Rick Incrocci

ISBN   978-0-7847-2127-8

          Library of Congress Cataloging-in-Publication Data

Loth, Paul.
  Bible stories for curious kids / by Paul J. Loth.
      p. cm.
  ISBN 978-0-7847-2127-8 (casebound)
  1. Bible stories, English. I. Title.
  BS551.3.L68 2010
  220.9'505--dc22

                              2010002164

15 14 13 12 11 10   1 2 3 4 5 6 7 8 9

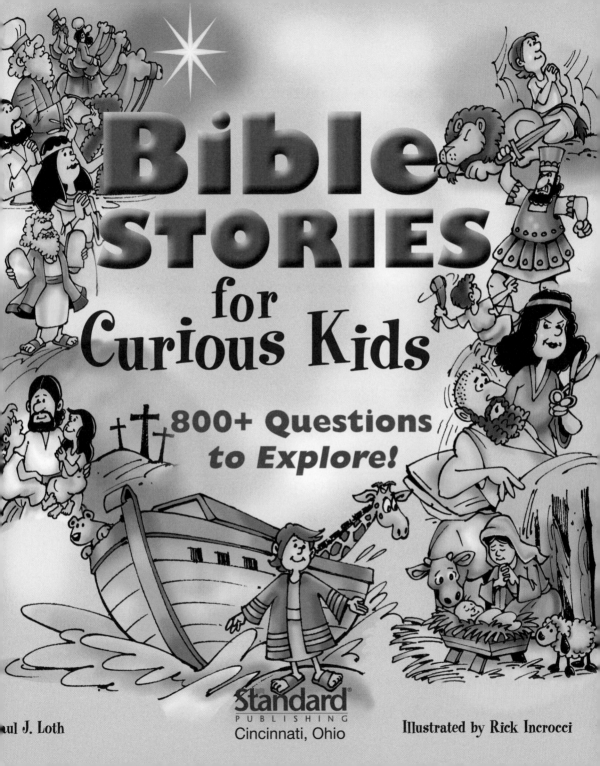

Bible
STORIES
for
Curious Kids

800+ Questions to Explore!

Standard
PUBLISHING
Cincinnati, Ohio

aul J. Loth

Illustrated by Rick Incrocci

Contents

Introduction: Questions, Questions, Questions............................ 10

The Old Testament

God Makes the World (*Genesis 1:1-19*) 13

The Perfect Garden (*Genesis 2:8-3:24*) 18

Noah and the Ark (*Genesis 6:1-7:9*) 21

A Beautiful Rainbow (*Genesis 7:10–9:17*) 25

Abraham Pleads for Sodom and Gomorrah (*Genesis 18:20–19:29*) 28

Abraham Has a Son (*Genesis 22:1-19*) 33

Jacob Tricks Isaac (*Genesis 27:1-45*) 36

Jacob and Uncle Laban (*Genesis 28:1–29:14*) 40

Joseph's Brothers Get Mad (*Genesis 37:1-36*) 43

God Helps Joseph (*Genesis 39:1–41:40*) 47

Jacob Moves to Egypt (*Genesis 41:41–46:34*) 52

Moses Is Born (*Exodus 1:8–2:10*) 57

Moses and the Burning Bush (*Exodus 3:1–4:14*) 61

Let My People Go (*Exodus 7:1–12:42*) 65

Moses Leads the People Out of Egypt (*Exodus 13:17–14:31*)........... 70

God Gives the Israelites Manna to Eat (*Exodus 16:1-36*) 74

Twelve Spies Check Out Their New Home (*Numbers 13:1–14:45*) .. 78

Rahab Joins God's Team (*Joshua 2:1-24*) 82

Jericho Is Destroyed (*Joshua 6:1-24*) 86

Gideon's Fleece (*Judges 6:1-40*) 90

Gideon's Army (*Judges 7:1-25*) 93

Samson Is the Strongest (*Judges 16:1-31*) 97

Ruth Believes (*Ruth 1:1–4:22*) 102

Samuel Hears God's Voice (*1 Samuel 1:1–3:21*) 106

God Feeds Elijah (*1 Kings 17:1-24*) 110

Elijah on Mount Carmel (*1 Kings 18:1-39*) 114

Elijah Runs Away (*1 Kings 19:1-18*) 118

Elijah Goes Home (*2 Kings 2:1-15*) 123

The Widow's Oil (*2 Kings 4:1-7*) 129

A Room for Elisha (*2 Kings 4:8-37*) 132

David Is Chosen King (*1 Samuel 16:1-13*) 137

David and Goliath (*1 Samuel 17*) 141

Wise King Solomon (*1 Kings 3:1-28*) 145

Queen Esther (*Esther 2:1–7:10*) 149

Job (*Job 1–2*) 154

Daniel Ate His Vegetables (*Daniel 1:1-20*) 158

The Fiery Furnace (*Daniel 3:1-30*) 161

Daniel and the Lions (*Daniel 6:1-28*) 165

Jonah (*Jonah 1–4*) 169

The New Testament

Jesus Is Born (*Luke 2:1-20*) 175

The Angel's Announcement (*Luke 2:8-16*) 178

The Wise Men Visit Jesus (*Mathew 2:1-20*) 182

Young Jesus at the Temple (*Luke 2:41-51*) 186

Jesus Is Baptized (*Matthew 3:1-17*) 190

Jesus Is Tempted (*Luke 4:1-13*) 194

Jesus Clears the Temple (*John 2:12-23*) 197

Jesus Calls His Disciples (*Luke 5:1-11*) 201

Jesus Saves the Wedding (*John 2:1-11*) 204

Jesus Heals the Paralyzed Man (*Mark 2:1-12*) 207

The Prodigal Son (*Luke 15:11-32*) 211

The Good Samaratin (*Luke 10:25-37*) 215

Jesus Heals Ten Lepers (*Luke 17:11-19*) 219

Jesus Has a Visitor—Nicodemus (*John 3:1-21*) 222

Jesus Stops a Storm (*Mark 4:35-41*) 226

Jesus Helps Jarius's Daughter (*Mark 5:21-43*) 230

Jesus Feeds 5,000 (*Matthew 14:13-21*) 234

Jesus Walks on Water (*Matthew 14:22-33*) 238

The Disciples Get a Show (*Matthew 17:1-13*) 242

Learning to Forgive (*Matthew 18:21-35*) 246

Jesus Helps a Blind Man *(John 9:1-41)* 250

The Woman at the Well *(John 4:1-42)* 254

Jesus Raises Lazarus *(John 11:1-44)* 258

Jesus Is Anointed with Oil *(John 12:1-11)* 262

Jesus Enters Jerusalem *(Mark 11:1-11)* 265

The Final Meal *(John 13:1-30)* 269

Jesus Came to Die *(John 18:1–19:16)* 273

Jesus Is Alive *(John 20:1-31)* 277

Jesus Helps Peter Fish *(John 21:1-22)*........................... 281

The Holy Spirit Comes *(Acts 2:1-41)* 285

Philip Chases a Chariot *(Acts 8:26-40)* 289

Saul Changes *(Acts 9:1-19)* 292

Saul Preaches About Jesus *(Acts 9:19-30)* 296

Peter Heals Aeneas and Dorcas *(Acts 9:32-42)* 300

Peter Learns That God Loves Everyone *(Acts 11:1-18)* 304

Peter Escapes from Prison *(Acts 12:1-19)* 308

A Great Earthquake *(Acts 16:16-40)*............................ 312

Paul's Nephew Helps *(Acts 23:1-35)* 316

Introduction

Questions, Questions, Questions

It always amazed me how my father kept in such close contact with his high school and college friends through the years. And whenever they came to visit, they seemed to tell the same stories every time. My father's friends would usually start with, "Remember that time . . . ?" and the story would begin—again!

About that time my sisters and I would want to know the details, since we hadn't been there and had a lot of questions about why they did things a certain way and what happened next. And, as we asked questions, we felt part of the story too—almost as if we had been there to see what happened along with my father and his friends.

I thought it was odd that my father would talk about the same events again and again with his friends. That is, until my college friends came to visit—and we talked about the same stories each time. Why did we do that? We had all been there. We knew what happened. We told the same stories because it made us feel good to talk about what happened. It made us feel as if everything were happening all over again.

Maybe that's why the Old Testament is filled with festivals to celebrate the times in which God did something special. And during the Passover meal, which was held in remembrance of how God rescued the people from slavery in Egypt, the children asked their fathers questions about what happened.

Jesus knew this. That's why almost everything he taught us was an answer to a question he was asked. And Jesus often answered questions he was asked with more questions.

Children do that too. Have you ever noticed how many questions young children can ask? Or how often you have to stop to think of the answer?

This book capitalizes on the way children think—through questions—and presents Bible stories in the form of questions and answers.

All the regular Bible stories are included. Each story begins with a brief introduction, and then the story is told by answering a series of questions. At the core of the book are the questions. By the questions, the reader is led through the story in a logical manner and in a way that gives the reader a complete picture of the story—much as I learned what happened to my father and his friends by asking them questions. In this open layout, each question is accompanied by a small illustration.

Instead of adding some application questions at the end of the story, these types of questions are integrated within the story, thus creating the potential for more interaction between the reader and the child. Stop and talk about these application questions with your children, and allow your children to add more questions of their own.

My objectives in writing this book are

- to present the Bible in a way that holds the listener's interest.

- to create an atmosphere that inspires interaction between listener and reader.

- to provide applications within the stories that help the reader relate the Bible to his or her daily life.

May this book make you feel like you were there when God touched the people's lives. And may God help your children to follow him and have their own stories with him.

Paul Loth, Ed.D.
Carol Stream, Illinois

The Old Testament

God Makes the World

Genesis 1:1-19

Have you ever thought about how everything was made? How the trees got planted, how the sun and moon appeared? How everything on Earth is just exactly *perfect*? The Bible answers that question in one word: God.

Did God make everything?

Yes. The Bible tells us that at first only God existed. There was nothing else. No land, no trees, no water. Nothing.

Where did God live?

He lived where he always lives. Everywhere. God does not have a body. God is a spirit. There is nowhere we can go in which God has not already been. Before the world was made, there was only one thing—God.

What did God make first?

God first made the heavens and the earth, but the earth had no shape. The heavens and earth were all together. God moved just above the water. It was dark.

So what did God do then?

What would you do if it was dark? Make light? That's what God did. He made light. Now, instead of everything being dark, there was light and there was dark. The light was called *day* and the dark was called *night*. The first day was now over.

If the earth had no form, how did it end up like it is now?

God made the sky. The sky separated the heavens from the earth. Now there was the sky, the heavens, and the earth. That was the end of the second day.

Did you say everything was water?

Yes, at first there was water above and below. But now the sky separated the water. Then God put dry land on the earth. That divided up the water into the different oceans and lakes we have now. He called the dry land *earth*, and he called the water *seas*.

So now there were oceans and land. What did the land look like?

The land was dry dirt, like it is before your mom or dad plants grass or a garden. God planted grass and plants and trees. There were a lot of good things to eat on earth, like fruit and vegetables. This was the end of day three.

How could grass and plants grow without sun?

Remember I said earlier that God made light? That's how we have different days. First it's dark, then it's light.

Then God made the sun and the moon. He made all the stars too.

Why was this so important?

Well, first, to give light to the earth during the day. Have you ever been out in the middle of the night and noticed how light it seems? Even the moon and the stars at night give light to the earth.

The sun and moon tell us when each day begins and ends. They also help us tell time and know when each week, month, and year ends. This was the end of the fourth day.

Wasn't the earth quiet?

Not for long! On the next day, day number five, God filled the oceans and lakes with fish and whales and sea mammals.

Then God filled the air and the trees with birds and everything that flies. It became very noisy very fast!

What about the land?

The land was filled on day six. First, the animals. Large animals, livestock, such as cows and bulls. Then wild animals, such as lions, tigers, and bears were created. And finally, all the animals that run along the ground. The land became very full and noisy in a hurry!

Did God create people then?

Yes. God made man to be just like him. He made man in the image of God. God named man "Adam" because he came from the ground.

What about girls?

God saw Adam with all the animals and birds and fish and trees. And he knew he would be lonely.

So God made woman. She would be Adam's partner and keep him company. Everyone needs a friend, right?

God thought of everything, didn't he?

Yes, he always does. In fact, after each day, God looked at everything he had made and made sure it was good. God still does that. He makes sure everything he makes for us is good.

The Perfect Garden

Genesis 2:8–3:24

A dam and Eve had it all. God made Adam. He was the first person on Earth. God knew that Adam would not be happy alone. He made Eve to be with him. The two of them could be together.

Then God put Adam and Eve in a beautiful garden—the garden of Eden.

What was the garden like?

It was perfect with all the beautiful trees, plants, animals, fruit. There was even a river watering the trees ging through the middle of the garden. Everything anyone would want.

Could Adam and Eve eat anything off the trees?

God told them they could eat anything in the garden. There was only one tree that Adam and Eve couldn't touch—the Tree of the Knowledge of Good and Evil. But there was no rule about anything else in the garden.

So what did Adam and Eve do?

Well, one day a snake started talking to Eve. That's right, started talking! In the garden the snake didn't slide on the ground. The snake was upright like all the other animals.

The snake asked Eve if she really was not able to eat from any tree in the garden.

What did Eve say?

She told the snake that they were allowed to eat from any tree but one. And that if they ate from that tree, they would die.

What did the snake tell her?

"You won't die," the snake told Eve. "You will be like God." So Eve took a bite of the fruit from the Tree of the Knowledge of Good and Evil.

What about Adam?

Eve took some fruit from the tree and gave it to Adam to eat too.

Were they okay?

Well, soon they heard God coming in the garden. So Adam and Eve went to hide from God.

Did God find them?

Of course. We can't hide from God. God asked them why they were hiding, and they said because they were naked and they were embarrassed. God knew they had disobeyed him.

Adam and Eve had to leave the garden right away. The snake had to crawl on his belly. And Adam and Eve had to work hard their entire lives.

They lost the perfect life—all because they disobeyed God and did the one thing that was wrong. The next time you think about disobeying God, think again!

Noah and the Ark

Genesis 6:1–7:9

Have you ever been sorry for something you have done? Something you thought was a good decision? Have you wished you had never done something? Wished you had done something different? That's how God felt about creating people. He was sorry he had done it.

Why was God so sorry he had created people?

God was angry that the world was in such bad shape. God said that every thought and action of people was bad. Does that sound familiar? A lot of people feel the same way today.

Weren't there any good people?

Yes. Noah. God said that the only one who obeyed him was Noah and his family.

So what did God do?

What would you do? God was sorry he had made people. He wanted to destroy everyone he had created and start over.

How was God going to do that?

God was going to flood the earth. Not only was God going to send rain from the sky but he would cause water to come up from the springs under the seas as well.

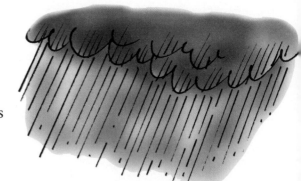

What about Noah and his family? Were they going to be caught in the flood too?

No. That's why God told Noah what he was going to do—to protect him. God wanted Noah to build a big boat, an ark. Noah and his family would live in the ark until the water was gone.

An ark? How big was it?

The ark Noah built was 450 feet long. To give you an idea of how long that is, think of a football field. A football field is 300 feet long from goal line to goal line. So the ark was one and a half football fields long!

And how tall?

It was 45 feet tall. That would be like a four-story building. If your school building is two stories high, that means the ark was double your school's height. The ark had a lower deck, a middle deck, and an upper deck.

Why such a big boat for one family?

Remember, it was not just Noah in the ark, but also his wife, his three sons, and their wives. So actually there were four families in the ark. In addition, two of every animal and creature entered the ark.

Was anyone else allowed in the ark?

No. God was planning to destroy all life on Earth and begin again. Once it started to rain, all the other people probably realized their mistake, but by then it was too late. They had already made their decision when they disobeyed God. It is important that we do what God wants and follow him.

A Beautiful Rainbow

Genesis 7:10–9:17

When was the last time it rained at your house? Did you go outside after the rain stopped? What did you see up in the sky? Did you see a rainbow? God put the rainbow up in the sky as a special promise for you.

Let's go back to the story of Noh and the ark.

How long did it rain while Noah and his family were in the ark?

God sent rain for 40 days and 40 nights. Rain came from the clouds in the sky. Water also came up from beneath the earth. You know what it's like when it rains one day, how water is everywhere. Just imagine what it was like after 40 days and 40 nights of rain.

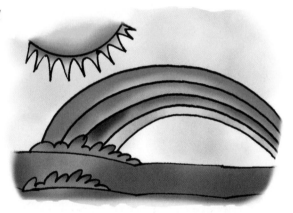

So how long did the water last on the earth?

Five months.

Then what happened?

At the end of five months, the water began to dry up. You need to realize that the water was more than 20 feet higher than the highest mountain. So, during the rainstorm, the ark was higher on the earth than even the mountains. The ark ended up landing on top of one of the mountains.

Noah opened the window in the ark and let a raven out.

Did the raven ever come back to the ark?

No, the raven flew around until the earth was dry. He never returned to the ark.

Did Noah and his family get out of the ark then?

No, Noah wanted to make sure that the water had dried from the earth, so he sent out a dove from the ark.

Did the dove come back to the ark?

Yes, the dove returned to the ark. That told Noah there was still water on the ground below the mountain.

So what did he do?

Noah waited a week and then sent the dove out again. This time the dove returned with an olive leaf in her mouth, so Noah knew the earth was dry. Noah and his family and all the animals left the ark.

What did Noah do then?

The first thing we should all do. He worshipped God and thanked him for keeping him and his family safe. God loved Noah, and he sent a promise in the form of a rainbow to Noah and people for all generations to come.

What did God promise with the rainbow?

God promised that he would never again destroy the world with a flood.

Abraham Pleads for Sodom and Gomorrah

Genesis 18:20–19:29

Do you know any places that are bad? Maybe a school or a neighborhood or part of a city? Sometimes it seems as if everything bad always happens in that place.

Sodom and Gomorrah were those kinds of places. In fact, Sodom and Gomorrah were so bad that Jesus even talked about them.

One day God was on Earth with two of his angels talking to Abraham. God wanted to see if Sodom and Gomorrah were as bad as people were saying. If they were, he would destoy them.

What did Abraham say?

Abraham asked God if he would still destroy Sodom and Gomorrah if he found in the city 50 good people—people who obeyed God.

What did God say?

God said, "I will spare the city if I find 50 good people."

Was Abraham happy with what God said?

No. He asked God another question. "What if only 40 good people are found there?" Abraham asked God.

What did God say to that?

"For the sake of forty, I will not destroy it," God answered.

What did Abraham say then?

"Don't get mad," Abraham said to God, "but what if only 30 good people can be found in Sodom?"

What did God say?

"I will not destroy it if I find 30 there."

Then what did Abraham say?

"I have been so bold," Abraham said, "what if only 20 can be found there?"

And how did God answer?

"For the sake of 20, I will not destroy the city," God told Abraham.

Did Abraham ask any more questions?

Yes. "Please don't be angry, but let me speak just once more," Abraham said to God. "What if only 10 good people could be found in the city?"

And what did God say?

"For the sake of 10," God told Abraham, "I will not destroy it."

So what did God do?

God sent two angels to see Lot, Abraham's nephew. Lot, his wife, and two daughters lived in Sodom. Lot invited them to stay in his home. But when they did, the men of the city tried to knock his door down to get at the angels who were visiting.

The angels told Lot to tell all the members of his family that God had decided the city was going to be destroyed.

Did Lot's family escape?

Yes. Lot and his wife and their two daughters all escaped. They ran to the next city, Zoar. They left at night, and by the time Lot's family got to Zoar, it was morning.

Did God destroy Sodom and Gomorrah then?

Yes. He sent sulfur and fire down from heaven. Both cities were destroyed. So were all the empty fields around the cities.

Were Lot and his family safe?

The angels told Lot and his family to hurry and run to the mountains and not to stop and not to look back.

But when her hometown was being destroyed, Lot's wife looked. And as soon as she did, she was turned into a pillar of salt.

When God tells us to do something or not to do something, we need to obey his commands. The people of Sodom and Gomorrah learned that. And so did Lot's wife. Have you learned to obey God too?

Abraham Has a Son

Genesis 22:1-19

Abraham was a special friend of God. God loved Abraham and told Abraham that his children would become many great nations. Even today, Abraham is known for his great faith and for believing in God.

One day, God came to talk to Abraham.

What did God tell Abraham?

God told Abraham that he and his wife, Sarah, would have a baby in a year.

Did Abraham's wife know?

Yes, Sarah knew. She was listening in the tent. She started to laugh. Abraham and Sarah were very old—much too old to be having children.

Did Sarah have the baby?

Yes. A year later, just as God had said. They named the baby Isaac, which means *laughter* because Sarah had laughed when God told Abraham about the baby.

Several years later what did God tell Abraham?

God told Abraham to take his son, Isaac, and go into the mountains. Abraham was to make a sacrifice and worship God.

So Abraham and Isaac and went into the mountains.

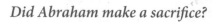

Did Abraham make a sacrifice?

He was preparing to. He and Isaac walked up to the spot where he was going to make the sacrifice. Abraham laid out the wood and built the altar for the sacrifice.

What was Abraham going to use for the sacrifice?

That's exactly what Isaac wanted to know. "The fire and the wood are here," Isaac said to his father, Abraham, "but where is the lamb for the sacrifice?"

"God will provide the lamb," Abraham answered. Actually, God had told Abraham to sacrifice his son, Isaac.

So what did Abraham do?

Abraham tied Isaac up and laid him on the wood. He prepared to kill his son and use him for the sacrifice.

Did he do it? Did Abraham kill Isaac?

No. Just then the angel of God called to Abraham. "Do not harm the boy," the angel said, "Now I know you fear God."

Nothing was more important to Abraham than God. He was willing to give up everything for the Lord. And God gave Abraham everything in return. Through Abraham's family the world would be blessed forever, all because Abraham obeyed God.

Jacob Tricks Isaac

Genesis 27:1-45

Isaac had two sons, Esau and Jacob. Like many brothers, they fought a lot. They were twins, but Esau was born first, so he had the right to the family blessing from Isaac. But Jacob and Esau's mother, Rebekah, loved Jacob best, and she wanted him to receive the blessing.

The years passed, and Isaac grew old and became very ill. He knew he would be dying soon, and it was time to bless his oldest son.

What did Isaac do?

One day he called Esau, who was a hunter, into his room. Isaac asked Esau to hunt for some meat and prepare a hot meal for him. Then Isaac would give Esau his blessing.

Was Rebekah happy for Esau?

No. When Rebekah overheard what her husband, Isaac, said to Esau, she immediately went to find her favorite son, Jacob. She told Jacob what Esau was about to do, and she came up with a plan to trick Isaac.

What was Rebekah's plan?

Since Esau was a hunter, it would take him a while to find and kill an animal to eat. Jacob, though, was a farmer and took care of flocks and animals. So Rebekah told Jacob to bring her two of the best goats in his flock. She would prepare Isaac's favorite meal for him.

Rebekah then gave the meal to Jacob to give to his father, Isaac, before Esau got back from hunting.

Wouldn't Isaac recognize that it was Jacob?

That's what Jacob asked his mother. Esau was a very hairy man, but Jacob had smooth skin. Jacob was afraid that his father would figure out it was Jacob and realize he was trying to trick him.

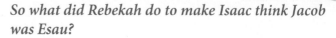

So what did Rebekah do to make Isaac think Jacob was Esau?

First, Jacob's mother took Esau's best clothes and had Jacob put them on. Then she took the skins of the goats that Jacob had brought to her and put those on his hands and on the back of his neck.

Did that fool his father?

Isaac asked Jacob who he was when he brought the food to him.

"I am Esau, your firstborn," Jacob answered his father.

Did Isaac believe him?

"Come near to me so I can touch you," Isaac said. So Jacob walked over close to his father, and Isaac felt Jacob.

"The voice is the voice of Jacob," Isaac said, "but the hands are the hands of Esau."

So did Jacob get Esau's blessing?

Isaac asked Jacob to come over and kiss him. When Isaac hugged Jacob, he smelled Esau's clothes on him. So Isaac gave Jacob the family blessing that was intended for Esau.

It was a special blessing. Isaac told Jacob that many nations would serve him and people would bow down to him. He also told Jacob that he would be stronger than his brother.

Did Esau know Jacob had tricked him out of his blessing?

Yes. Right after Isaac blessed Jacob, Esau came home from hunting. He fixed his father's favorite meal and came in to receive his blessing.

What did his father say?

Isaac asked Esau who he was and Esau said, "I am your son, Esau."

Isaac figured out then that Jacob had tricked him and taken his brother's blessing. Even though Jacob had received the blessing intended for Esau, he would have a very difficult life and end up having many people trick him and make him unhappy, even his own children.

Jacob got what he wanted by cheating, but he would end up getting what he deserved. Other people would treat Jacob the same way he had treated Esau. As Jesus would say many years later, "Do unto others as you would have them do unto you." The Golden Rule from Jesus is also the best way to live our lives. Jacob would have been wise to follow that too.

Jacob and Uncle Laban

Genesis 28:1–29:14

Jacob had tricked his brother, Esau. He ended up getting the family blessing instead of Esau. But now Jacob and Esau's father, Isaac, had died. Jacob's mother, Rebekah, was afraid Esau might try to hurt Jacob.

So what did Rebekah do?

Rebekah sent Jacob to her brother, Laban. Partway there, Jacob stopped to rest for the night.

What happened during the night?

Jacob had a dream. In the dream, there was a ladder between Jacob and Heaven. Angels were climbing up and down the ladder.

God spoke to Jacob. He told Jacob that this place was special and would be the land for all of Jacob's family. God also told Jacob, "I am with you and will watch over you wherever you go, and I will bring you back to this land. I will not leave you."

So what did Jacob do?

Jacob made a special altar to God and poured oil on the rock he had used as a pillow. He made a promise to God that he would follow him. Jacob named the place Bethel, which means "House of God."

Then did Jacob go see his uncle Laban?

Yes. When Jacob got near Laban's house, he saw several flocks of sheep and a well filled with water for the sheep.

Did Jacob know where Laban lived?

No. But he saw some men there with their sheep. Jacob asked them if they knew Laban.

"Yes, we know him," they told Jacob, "and here comes his daughter, Rachel, with his sheep."

Did Jacob talk to Rachel?

Yes. He told her that he was her father's nephew. Jacob then rolled the stone away from the mouth of the well and helped Rachel water the sheep.

What did Rachel do?

She ran to get her father, Laban, Jacob's uncle.

Did Laban come to meet Jacob?

Yes. Laban invited Jacob to stay with him. Jacob helped Laban take care of his sheep.

Joseph's Brothers Get Mad

Genesis 37:1-36

Do you get along with your brothers? Always? Well, Joseph and his brothers didn't get along. Joseph kept saying and doing things that upset them.

What did Joseph do?

One day, when Joseph was 17, he was out with his brothers taking care of the sheep. When he came back home, Joseph told his father, Jacob, bad things about his brothers.

Do you like it when your brothers or friends tell on you?

What did his father do?

Jacob made a coat for Joseph. It was a beautiful coat. That made Joseph's brothers feel like Joseph was their father's favorite. Which was true, of course.

Is that why Joseph's brothers didn't like him?

One reason. Then Joseph had a dream one day. His dream was that his sheaf of grain stood upright, and his brothers' sheaves of grain were bent over, bowing to him.

Did Joseph tell the dream to his brothers?

Yes, he did. He told the dream to his father too. They were all very upset with Joseph. In Joseph's dream, it was like his brothers were his slaves.

So what did Joseph's brothers do?

One day the brothers were out taking care of the sheep. Jacob, their father, told Joseph to go find them.

Did Joseph find them?

Joseph went to where their father said they would be with the sheep. But he didn't find them there. The field was empty. No one was there.

So what did Joseph do?

Joseph saw a man there in the field and Joseph asked the man if he had seen his brothers. He told Joseph that they had left and had gone to a town named Dothan.

Did Joseph find his brothers there?

Yes. But they saw him coming. His brothers said, "Here comes that dreamer. Let's take care of him."

It's okay to be mad (that's normal), but we should never make plans to be mean to others. That makes God sad.

What did Joseph's brothers do?

They grabbed Joseph and tore off his coat. They were going to kill him and throw him into a well. But they didn't.

Why didn't the brothers kill Joseph?

One of the brothers, Reuben, said that they should just throw him in the well unharmed. So that's what they did. Reuben was hoping to come back later and rescue Joseph.

Did Reuben rescue him?

No. While Joseph's brothers were trying to decide what to do with Joseph, a caravan of slave traders came by. Another brother, Judah, told the others that they should just sell Joseph to the slave traders. So that's what they did.

God Helps Joseph

Genesis 39:1–41:40

After being sold by his brothers into slavery, Joseph was taken to Egypt. There Joseph was sold to Potiphar, who was the captain of the guard, one of the leading officials of the king of Egypt.

What did Joseph do for Potiphar?

He was a servant for Potiphar's household. Potiphar trusted Joseph so much that he placed him in charge of the entire house.

Did Joseph do a good job as head of the household?

Yes. But then one day Potiphar's wife tried to get Joseph to disobey Potiphar and do something he knew was wrong. But Joseph said no.

Do your friends ever try to get you to do the wrong thing?

So what did she do?

Joseph kept doing his best to avoid Potiphar's wife. One day she caught up to him and grabbed his cloak and tried to get him to disobey God. Joseph ran out of the house, but Potiphar's wife held on to his cloak.

What did she do with Joseph's cloak?

Potiphar's wife waited until her husband got home. Then she lied to get Joseph in trouble. Have you ever done that?

What did Potiphar do?

He was very upset. He had Joseph thrown into jail. Joseph didn't even have a chance to explain what really happened. And who would have believed a slave over the wife of the captain of the guard in Egypt?

So what happened to Joseph in jail?

Joseph tried to get people to listen to him. Although he told everyone he had done nothing wrong and he shouldn't be in jail, no one would listen to him. But the jail warden liked Joseph and gave him freedom in jail.

Joseph made two new friends in prison. One had been a chief baker and the other a chief cupbearer before they were imprisoned.

How did Joseph help these friends?

One night they both had dreams. You know, the kind of dreams that seemed real.

Joseph told them he had a lot of experience with dreams, so they both told him about their dreams and he told them what they meant.

What were the dreams?

The chief cupbearer had a dream that there were grapes on a vine. He took the grapes and made them into wine and gave the wine to the king.

Joseph told him that the dream meant he would soon get his job back as the chief cupbearer to the king.

"And when you do," Joseph told him, "be sure to tell him about me. Tell him that I didn't do anything wrong and should not be in prison."

What about the chief baker's dream?

The chief baker had a dream that he had three baskets of bread. Birds flew by and ate the bread in the top basket so there was nothing left.

Joseph told him that his dream meant he would die.

Was Joseph right?

Yes. Three days later the chief cupbearer was returned to his job with the king. And the chief baker died.

Did the chief cupbearer remember to tell the king about Joseph?

No, he forgot.

But then one day the king had a terrible dream. It was so upsetting he couldn't sleep.

So what did the king do?

The king called all the wise men and advisers of the kingdom in to help him. He told them all his dream, but they couldn't figure it out.

Then the chief cupbearer remembered Joseph. "When I was in prison," he told the king, "there was a young Hebrew there with us. We told him our dreams, and he told us what they meant. And things turned out exactly as he told us."

What did the king say?

He said to bring Joseph to him. So they let Joseph out of jail and got him cleaned up and ready to appear befoe the king.

Joseph listened to the king's dreams. Then he told him what the dreams meant. "There will be seven years of a great economy and lots of food," Joseph told the king, "but that will be followed by seven years of hunger and starvation."

Did the king believe Joseph?

Yes. In fact he asked Joseph what he thought he should do. Joseph told him to store all the food during the first seven years, and then he would have food for the seven years of starvation.

The king liked the idea so much he put Joseph in charge of the palace and the nation. He told everyone to do whatever Joseph told them to do. Joseph was in charge of everyone but the king.

Joseph did the right thing and obeyed God. Even though he was wrongly punished, Joseph stayed true to God. And God took care of Joseph. If we continue to believe what God tells us, like Joseph did, God will do great things with us and take care of us too.

Jacob Moves to Egypt

Genesis 41:41–46:34

Jacob and his sons were hungry. They couldn't find food anywhere. One day Jacob heard that there was food in Egypt. The Egyptians had been storing food, and now they had food to give out to people who were hungry.

What did Jacob do?

Jacob told his sons, "I have heard that there is grain in Egypt. Go down there and buy some for us, so that we may live."

So did they go to Egypt?

Ten of Jacob's sons went to Egypt to get food. Joseph was in charge of the food in Egypt. Joseph was their brother. They thought Joseph was dead.

They had to meet with Joseph to ask for food.

Did they know who Joseph was?

No, but Joseph knew them. He asked them about their father and their younger brother, Benjamin.

Joseph's brothers had been mean to him. But instead of being mean back, Joseph was nice to his brothers at first.

What did Joseph do?

Joseph wanted to see his brother Benjamin, so he told his brothers he thought they were spies. He arrested one of the brothers, Simeon, and put him in jail.

Joseph told them he would let Simeon go when they brought Benjamin back to see him. Benjamin and Joseph had the same mother so they were very close.

Did Joseph ever give them any food?

Yes, he filled their bags with food and they went back home. Everyone, that is, but Simeon.

What did their father, Jacob, say?

Jacob was very upset. He thought Joseph was dead. And now his sons told him he had to send Benjamin to Egypt. He said, "My son will not go down there with you." He was afraid of losing Benjamin too.

So what happened then?

There continued to be a problem. Jacob and his sons ran out of food again.

Jacob wanted his sons to go back to Egypt to get more food. But his sons told him they had to take Benjamin. So Jacob finally agreed, and Benjamin traveled to Egypt with them.

Did they see Joseph?

Yes. Joseph arranged for a special meal at his home for the brothers and Benjamin. When Joseph saw Benjamin, he was so happy, he went into another room and cried tears of joy. But he still did not tell them who he was.

Did Joseph give them more food?

Yes, he filled up their bags with food and then he sent them back. Joseph also had his personal silver cup put in Benjamin's pack.

Why did Joseph do that?

He wanted to test his brothers and see if they had changed. After Joseph's brothers left to go home, Joseph sent men after them and accused them of stealing his silver cup. When they checked the brothers' bags, they found the silver cup in Benjamin's bag.

Joseph said he was going to make Benjamin his slave as punishment for stealing his cup.

What did the brothers say?

They begged Joseph not to keep Benjamin. His brother Judah offered to stay with Joseph in place of Benjamin. They explained how Jacob felt about Benjamin and how upset he would be if Benjamin did not come home with them.

What did Joseph say?

Joseph had everyone other than his brothers leave the room. Then he hugged his brothers and said, "I am Joseph!" He explained everything that God had done, how God had put him in a position in Egypt so he could help them.

What did the brothers do?

At first, his brothers were scared. A long time ago Joseph's brothers had tried to kill him. They ended up selling him as a slave instead. They were afraid that Joseph would be mean to them now that he was head of all Egypt.

But Joseph explained that God used what they did to help Joseph. Has that ever happened to you? Sometimes terrible things happen (such as having to move or change schools) and God uses them to do something great. That's what God did with Joseph.

What happened to Joseph's brothers?

Pharaoh, the king of Egypt, heard about Joseph's brothers and his father and told Joseph to bring them to Egypt. He would give them the best place to live and the best of everything he had.

So Jacob and his sons moved to Egypt. Jacob was so excited to see his son again and to be together as a family.

Moses Is Born

Exodus 1:8–2:10

The Egyptians were worried. The people of Israel had been their slaves for 400 years. But the Israelites were growing faster than the Egyptians. Soon there would be more Israelites than Egyptians living in Egypt.

Why would that be a problem?

The Egyptians were concerned the Israelites would take over the country.

So what did they do about it?

Pharaoh, the king of Egypt, made a rule that all baby boys should be killed.

Did that work?

No. The women helping deliver the babies loved God. And, like everyone who loves God, they did what God wanted and let the babies live.

What did the king do then?

The king made another rule. All baby boys who were born should be thrown into the Nile River.

Did everyone do that?

Not everyone. One mother decided to hide her beautiful baby boy.

How long did she hide him?

For three months. Then, when she couldn't hide him any longer, she put her baby in a basket and hid him under some reeds in the river.

She just left him in the river?

She had her daughter stand nearby and watch the baby to make sure he was okay.

What happened?

Soon the daughter of Pharaoh, the king of Egypt, came by. When she walked down to the edge of the river, she found the basket.

Did Moses' sister say anything to her?

Yes. She asked Pharaoh's daughter if she
wanted her to get a woman to nurse the
baby for her.

What did Pharaoh's daughter say?

She said, "Yes, that would be nice.
Thank you."

So the girl went to get her mother,
who was, of course, the baby's
mother.

What happened to the baby?

When he was ready, his mother gave him to
Pharaoh's daughter to raise as her own son.
She named him "Moses" because she drew
him out of the water.

Moses became a great leader for the nation of
Israel. He ended up leading the Israelites out
of Egypt.

Moses and the Burning Bush

Exodus 3:1–4:17

Moses was a shepherd. He worked with his father-in-law, Jethro, and helped him take care of his flocks. One day Moses led his sheep to the foot of the mountain called Horeb. Something happened on Mount Horeb that would change Moses' life forever.

What happened on Mount Horeb?

Moses saw a burning bush. The bush was burning, but it wasn't burning up. It just kept burning.

What did Moses do?

Moses walked over to see the bush. He wanted to see why the bush just kept burning.

What did he find out?

He found out that God was there. "Moses! Moses!" God said.

What did Moses say?

"Here I am," Moses said.

"Take your sandals off," God told Moses. "The place where you are standing is holy ground."

Then what did God say?

God told Moses that he was God and he was going to free the Israelites from slavery in Egypt. When Moses found out that it was God, he was afraid to look at God so he hid his face. God told Moses he had chosen him to lead the people of Israel out of Egypt.

Did Moses tell God he would do it?

No. Moses was scared. He had a lot of excuses, from "the people won't listen to me" to "I'm not good enough."

Do you give God excuses when he tells you he wants you to do a job? God wants us to be willing to do what he wants. He will help us.

What did God say?

God told Moses to throw his staff down on the ground. Shepherds took a staff with them everywhere. They used it to walk with and to guide the sheep.

Did Moses do that?

Yes. As soon as he threw his staff down on the ground, it became a snake. Moses was horrified and ran away. Snakes are very dangerous.

What happened next?

God told Moses to pick up the
snake by the tail. When he did,
it turned back into his staff
again.

So Moses agreed to do what God wanted?

Not quite. "Oh, Lord," said Moses. "Please send
someone." Moses was afraid he wasn't a good
enough public speaker.

What did God say?

God told Moses that his brother, Aaron,
would be coming to meet him. God would
give messages to Moses and Aaron would
speak the messages to the people. Aaron
would be Moses' mouth.

So that is what happened: Moses and Aaron
led the people out of Egypt and God did great
things through them.

Let My People Go

Exodus 7:1–12:42

The people of Israel were slaves in Egypt. But the Israelites were God's people. God wanted the Israelites to be free. Moses was the leader of the people of Israel. God told Moses to go to Pharaoh, the king of Egypt, and tell him to let the Israelites leave Egypt.

Did Pharaoh let the Israelites go?

No. Pharaoh just laughed at Moses and Aaron, Moses' brother, when they told him that God said to let the Israelites go.

So what did Moses do?

He threw his staff down to the ground. It became a snake.

What did Pharaoh say to that?

Pharaoh called out his magicians, and they threw their staffs down on the ground. Their staffs became snakes also. But Aaron's snake swallowed Pharaoh's magicians' snakes.

Did that make Pharaoh change his mind?

No. The next day Moses met Pharaoh at the Nile River. He told him that God was going to change the Nile River to blood. All the fish would die and the water would be bad.

Aaron stretched out his staff over the river and turned it to blood.

Did that convince Pharaoh?

No, he just turned around and walked back to the palace.

What did Moses and Aaron do then?

A week later Moses told Pharaoh that God would send frogs to Egypt. The nation would be filled with frogs. There would be frogs in people's homes, in every building, and the land would be covered with frogs.

Did that convince Pharaoh?

Yes. He called Moses and Aaron to the palace. He told them to get rid of the frogs and he would let the Israelites leave.

So Moses and Aaron got rid of the frogs. But guess what? You're right. Pharaoh didn't let the people go after all.

Did Moses and Aaron do anything else to Pharaoh?

Oh, yes. Aaron struck the ground with his staff. When he did, gnats appeared everywhere. They were on everything and everybody, even all the animals. And after the gnats, they sent flies.

Even Pharaoh's advisers told him to let the Israelites go. So Pharaoh told Moses to remove the flies and he would let the Israelites leave. Moses removed the flies, but guess what? Pharaoh changed his mind again.

So what did Moses and Aaron do next?

They told Pharaoh that all the animals of the Egyptians would die. But still he wouldn't let the people of Israel go.

Did Moses and Aaron do anything else?

Moses took ashes from the furnace and threw them in the air. The ashes turned into soot in the air and made boils on people and animals.

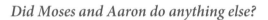

What did Pharaoh say then?

Pharaoh's advisers couldn't even meet with Moses and Aaron because they were covered with boils.

But Pharaoh still wasn't convinced. So Moses sent hail. Large hailstones fell everywhere. It was the worst hailstorm ever in the land of Egypt. After that, God sent locusts. The entire nation of Egypt was filled with them.

Did Pharaoh let the Israelites leave then?

Again, Pharaoh said he would let them go but changed his mind after Moses got rid of the locusts. So Moses and Aaron told him they would make Egypt dark. There would be no sun at all. Everything would be dark for three days.

Finally, Pharaoh had had enough. The nation of Egypt was being destroyed.

So what did Pharaoh do?

He called Moses and Aaron to the palace and told them to get the Israelites and leave.

"I never want to see your face again," Pharaoh told Moses.

Moses said that was fine. But God would do one more thing to make sure Pharaoh let the people go.

What was that?

The firstborn child of every Egyptian family would die. But the children of Israel were safe. All they had to do was to put the blood of a lamb on their doorposts. Then the angel of death would pass over the house. People still celebrate this night as Passover.

The next day the Israelites left Egypt for good. God had taken care of them. He proved he is more powerful than any king of any nation on Earth.

Moses Leads the People Out of Egypt

Exodus 13:17–14:31

The Israelites were finally free! They had been slaves in Egypt for more than 400 years. But they were now leaving. God did great things in Egypt to get Pharaoh, the king of Egypt, to let the people of Israel leave. And the day finally came for them to leave Egypt and go to their new home. They took everything they had, even the bones of Joseph.

Why did they take Joseph's bones?

Joseph was the son of Jacob who first came to Egypt. He was a leader in Egypt when the rest of Jacob's family came to stay there. Joseph knew that God would lead the people out of Egypt. When they did, Joseph wanted his bones to be taken with them and buried in the new land.

How did they know which way to go?

God sent a pillar of cloud. The pillar went in front of the Israelites to show them which way to go.

Could they see the cloud at night?

No. At night God led the Israelites with a pillar of fire. So they could travel at night or during the day.

What happened?

After the Israelites had left Egypt, Pharaoh changed his mind. He didn't like losing all those free workers.

So what did Pharaoh do?

Pharaoh told his entire army to go after the Israelites. He wanted them to catch the people who had left Egypt and bring them back.

Did they catch them?

Yes, the armies of Egypt caught up to the Israelites just before they got to the Red Sea.

Were the Israelites scared?

Yes. They yelled at Moses, "Why did you bring us out to the desert to die? We were better off as slaves in Egypt."

What did Moses do?

The angel of God moved behind the Israelites to protect them from the Egyptian armies. Also, the pillar of cloud that had been leading the Israelites moved behind them and in front of the Egyptians. So the people of Israel were protected and safe.

Then Moses put his staff over the Red Sea and said, "Do not be afraid. Stand still, and you will see the Lord save you today. The Lord will fight for you; you need only to be still."

What happened to the Red Sea?

The Lord sent a strong wind, and all night long the wind blew. By morning the waters had been parted and there was a dry path right in the middle of the sea.

Did the Israelites go through it?

Yes. First thing in the morning, all the people of Israel walked through the middle of the Red Sea on dry land. Like God said, all they had to do was trust him and be silent and God would protect them.

The next time you have a problem, remember that. Be silent and trust God and watch him save you!

What did the Egyptians do?

The Egyptian armies followed them. But God gave them problems. Their chariot wheels fell off and they got stuck.

Then God told Moses to put his staff over the Red Sea. By morning the water had gone back to what it was like before. God had saved the Israelites!

God Gives the Israelites Manna to Eat

Exodus 16:1-36

God had saved the people of Israel—again. He rescued them from slavery in Egypt. Then God saved them when the Egyptians chased them into the Red Sea. But the Israelites were still not happy. They complained to Moses again.

Do you ever do that? Are you a complainer too?

What were the Israelites complaining about?

The people of Israel had to travel through a desert—the Desert of Sin. They didn't have food to eat and they were hungry. Do you ever get cranky when you are hungry?

What did they want to do instead?

The Israelites told Moses they liked it better when they were slaves in Egypt. At least there they had food to eat. God should have let them stay in Egypt and die there.

So what did God do?

God told Moses he would send meat to the people of Israel in the evening and bread to the people every morning.

Did Moses tell the Israelites?

Yes, he gathered all the people together to tell them that God had heard them complaining and was going to give them food.

Aaron told the people about the meat in the evening and the bread in the morning. As Aaron was talking, the Israelites looked out over the desert and saw God there in a cloud.

What happened that night?

There was quail on the ground. The entire camp was covered with the quail.

What about the next morning?

The ground was covered with something that looked like dew.

What was it?

That's what the Israelites asked Moses. "It is the bread God has given you to eat," Moses said.

The people called the bread *manna*, which means, "What is it?" It was white and tasted like wafers made with honey.

Did the Israelites get the manna every morning?

Yes. Every morning but the Sabbath (Saturday). The Sabbath was the Lord's Day, and no work was to be done on that special day. But God sent the manna every other morning. The people were supposed to only collect enough manna for that day, about two quarts of manna for each person in the family. It would spoil after that. Then the next morning God sent more manna for them to eat.

Did everyone do that?

Everyone collected manna for their family, yes. But some people tried to save the manna until the next day.

What happened?

Just as Moses said, the manna spoiled and started to stink. Then everyone knew that those people had disobeyed God.

But what about Saturday or the Sabbath?

God sent enough manna to last two days and the manna would not spoil on that day. But guess what? Some of the Israelites still went out and looked for more manna on Saturday morning!

God had provided more food than the Israelites needed every day. But still they disobeyed him and tried to get more. Sounds familiar, doesn't it? If we trust God and do what he says, he will take care of us too.

Twelve Spies Check Out Their New Home

Numbers 13:1–14:45

The time had finally come. God had rescued his people, the Israelites, from being slaves in Egypt. He then rescued them from the Egyptians. And God led them through the desert.

And now the people of Israel were at the Jordan River. All they needed to do was cross the river and take over the land God had promised them. But first Moses needed to check out the land and see how difficult it would be to take it over.

How did Moses do that?

First, Moses picked one person from every tribe in Israel. The people had been divided into twelve families, or tribes, according to the sons of Jacob. So Moses picked one person, one leader, from each tribe to go into the new land and see what it was like.

They were spies?

Yes, you could call them that. Before they left, Moses told them what to look for. They were to see what they thought of the land, what it looked like, if the plants and fruit were good, what the people living there were like. Moses also wanted them to bring back some fruit.

Did they do that?

Yes. The twelve men spent 40 days, more than a month, in the land. When they came back, two of them were carrying a branch of fruit from one of the trees.

What did they tell Moses when they came back?

Well, actually they met with all the people of Israel. They told them how wonderful the land was and what great fruit and vegetables were growing there. They also told them how big and strong the people were and how they felt like grasshoppers in comparison to them.

So they did not want to go into the land?

Well, ten of them did not. But Caleb, one of the spies, had faith in God. He remembered how God had rescued them from Egypt, saved them at the Red Sea, and brought them through the desert. He had faith that God would take care of them.

What did the Israelites do?

The people of Israel were scared. They yelled at Moses and Aaron and told them that they were being brought out to die in the desert.

What did Moses say?

Moses and Aaron fell on their faces in front of the Israelites. Caleb and Joshua, the two spies who wanted to go into the land, pleaded with the people of Israel. "If the Lord is pleased with us, he will lead us into the land," they said. "The Lord is with us. Do not be afraid of the people of the land."

So what did the people of Israel do?

They wanted to stone Joshua and Caleb. When you get scared, don't you do strange things too? It's better to believe than to get scared.

Just then the Lord appeared in the Tent of Meeting, the special tent in which God appeared to Moses. God told Moses he was going to kill all the Israelites and start over with Moses.

Moses talked God out of it. But the people of Israel would not go into the special land.

Did Moses tell the Israelites?

Yes. They were upset. They realized they had made a mistake—the mistake of disobeying God and not trusting him.

What did the Israelites do?

The next morning the Israelites came to see Moses. "We have sinned," they told Moses. "We will go into the land now."

"Do not go into the land," Moses told them. "The Lord is not with you."

So did they go into the land?

The Israelites tried, but the people who lived there chased them all the way back to the camp. God had told them to obey him, and they said no. Now they had to live with the pain of disobeying God.

When God tells you to do somethng, do it the *first* time!

Rahab Joins God's Team

Joshua 2:1-24

The Israelites had made it through the wilderness—twice! God saved them from being slaves and kept them safe. This was the second time they were ready to go into the special land God had promised them. The first time Moses sent spies into the land, they became scared and didn't want to go into the land.

This time, Joshua was in charge of the people of Israel. He was not going to make the same mistake.

What did Joshua do?

Joshua sent two spies to check out the land. He especially wanted the spies to look at the city of Jericho. Jericho was a big city with tall walls all around it.

Where did the spies stay?

They stayed in the home of a woman named Rahab.

Were the spies safe there?

They thought they would be safe, but the king of Jericho found out about the spies. He called Rahab and told her to bring the spies out from her house.

What did Rahab do?

First, Rahab took the men up to her rooftop. She hid them under stalks of flax she had stored there.

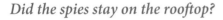

Did the spies stay on the rooftop?

Yes. Then Rahab told the king, "The men did come to me, but I did not know where they had come from. At dusk, when it was time to close the city gate, the men left. I don't know which way they went. Go after them quickly. You might catch up with them."

Did the men run after them?

Yes, of course, but the spies were still hiding on Rahab's rooftop.

What did Rahab do with the Israelite men?

She told them she believed God. And she knew that the Israelites were going to take over their land. But when the Israelites came into the land, she wanted them to keep her and her family safe.

So how were they going to keep Rahab's family safe?

Rahab's house was part of the wall of the city of Jericho. The men told Rahab to put a scarlet cord in her window. When the Israelites came into the land, they would look for the cord and keep the people of that house safe.

How did the spies get out safely?

Rahab let them out by a rope through her window. Since her house was part of the wall, the two men were able to get away without having to go through the city gate.

Did the spies go back then?

Yes. Rahab told them to go into the hills and wait three days until the men from Jericho who were chasing them had come back to the city. Then they could go back to their camp.

Did the spies tell Joshua what happened?

Yes. The spies especially told Joshua about Rahab and everything she said, including how Rahab believed in God and knew that God would give the Israelites the land. Even the enemies like Rahab believed in God. Rahab put her life in danger because she wanted to be on God's side.

God's side is always the winning side. What side are you on?

Jericho Is Destroyed

Joshua 6:1-24

Jericho was a very strong city. There was a tall wall all around it, and the only way into the city was through the city gate. The people of Jericho could see the Israelites coming, and they were ready to protect themselves.

What did the Israelites do?

God defeated the city of Jericho. Seven priests carrying trumpets of rams' horns marched around the city of Jericho in front of the ark of God. The armed guard marched in front of the priests, and the rear guard marched behind the priests and the ark.

What was the ark of God?

The ark of God was the place where God was present. It contained the Ten Commandments of God given to Moses, the Law of God, and was the special place of God. When the Israelites were with the Ark of God, they were with God.

What happened after they marched around the city of Jericho?

After the priests and army of Israel marched around the city of Jericho, they went back to their camp and spent the night.

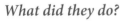

Did they do anything the next day?

Yes. Early in the morning Joshua lined up the armed guard first. Then came the priests with their trumpets and the ark of God, followed by the rear guard.

What did they do?

The priests carried their trumpets while they all marched around the city, and then they returned to their camp and stayed the night.

Did the Israelites do the same thing the next day?

Exactly the same thing. Same people. Same lineup. Same trumpets. Six days in a row Joshua led the people of Israel around the city of Jericho. And each day, the Israelites returned to their camp to spend the night.

What happened on the seventh day?

Joshua got everyone up at the beginning of the day, as the sun was coming up. They lined up as they had every day before that, with the armed guard, the priests, and the ark of God, followed by the rear guard. But, after marching around the city, the Israelites did not go back to the camp. They marched around the city again. They marched around the city *seven* times.

What happened after the seventh time around the city?

The priests sounded the trumpets and Joshua said, "Shout! For the Lord has given you the city!"

Did the people shout?

Yes! The trumpets sounded. Then the people shouted. And the mighty walls of the city of Jericho fell down!

What did the Israelites do?

The first thing they did was to bring out Rahab and her family. Rahab had hidden the spies when they came in to see the land. Rahab had chosen to follow God. And now she and her family were kept safe too.

What about the rest of the city of Jericho?

The Israelites ran into the city and destroyed it. The entire city was burned. Jericho did not follow and obey God. So God did not want anything to remain.

When you decided to follow God, you did not want to keep anything from the past, did you? It's best to give God all your attention and destroy the past ways of disobeying him. That's what the Israelites did too.

Gideon's Fleece

Judges 6:1-40

The Israelites did not obey God, so God punished them. God let another nation take over Israel. He wanted the people of Israel to learn to obey him. God wanted the people of Israel to love and follow him again.

God wanted someone to lead the Israelites. He wanted a leader to win the battles. So one day the angel of the Lord came to talk to Gideon.

What did the angel say to Gideon?

"The Lord is with you, mighty warrior," the angel said.

"Give me a sign that it really is the Lord talking to me," Gideon said to the angel.

What did Gideon do?

Gideon went inside and prepared some meat and bread. Then he brought it out to the angel.

What did the angel tell Gideon to do?

The angel told Gideon to put the meat and bread on a rock.

Then what did the angel do?

The angel touched the meat with the end of his staff. Fire came out of the rock and burned up the meat. This was a sign for Gideon.

So what did Gideon do then?

Gideon wanted to know for sure that it was God who was speaking to him.

Gideon put a fleece of wool out overnight. He told God that if, in the morning, the wool was wet and the ground is dry, then he would know it was truly God who was speaking to him.

So what happened?

When Gideon woke in the morning, the fleece of wool was soaked. Gideon picked it up and squeezed out a bowl of water. But the ground around it was dry.

So was Gideon convinced?

Gideon had one more request. "This time," Gideon said, "I want the fleece to be dry but the ground around it to be wet."

What happened?

Just as Gideon had said, when he got up in the morning, the ground was wet with morning dew. But the fleece was dry.

Gideon had his answer. Now it was Gideon's time to obey God and to do what he said. Just like all of us should do.

Gideon's Army

Judges 7:1-25

It was time to fight back. The nation of Israel had been taken over by the nation of Midian. But the land of Israel was God's land. It was the land God had given to the Israelites. And now the Israelites were taking the land back.

But God wanted the Israelites to know that he was going to win the battle. So God told Gideon there were too many people in the army. The army needed to be smaller so the people would know it was God who was going to win, not them.

How did Gideon make the army smaller?

The first thing Gideon did was to tell the men in the army that whoever was scared could go home.

Did anyone leave?

Yes, 22,000 men left to go home. There were 10,000 men left.

Was the army still too large?

Yes. So God told Gideon to take the army down to the river and he would watch them each get a drink. This would be God's way of determining which men wold stay to fight.

How did the men take a drink?

Well, some of the men got down on their knees and lapped up the water with their toungues like dogs.

How did the others take a drink?

Three hundred men lapped the water to their mouths using their hands.

What was God's decision after watching the men drink the water?

The men who got down on their knees to drink were told to go back to the tents in the camp.

What about the 300 men who lapped the water with their hands?

They were the ones Gideon took into battle against the army from Midian. Yes, you're right, only 300 men were going into battle with Gideon.

How did Gideon arm the men?

Gideon gave each of the men a trumpet and an empty jar with a torch inside. Then he divided the 300 men into three groups of 100 men each.

What did Gideon tell them to do?

He told the three groups of men to circle the camp and watch him. At just the right moment, they were to all blow their trumpets and shout, "For God and for Gideon," and smash the jars they had in their hands.

Did they do that?

Yes, they circled the camp of the army of Midian and waited until the guard changed. Then Gideon blew his trumpet. Just then they all blew their trumpets and shouted.

What happened to the soldiers from Midian?

They ran for their lives. There were so many of them running that Gideon needed to get help from other Israelites to chase them all down. God had won the battle. All Gideon and the 300 men needed to do was trust him.

Samson Is the Strongest

Judges 16:1-31

Who is the strongest man you know? No one can beat him, can they? Do you know what makes him so strong? Does he use his strength for good or for bad?

A long time ago, a man named Samson was the strongest man alive. Samson used his strength to help the people of Israel. He wanted to help God's people and fight against the enemies of God. When you are strong, you will want to help God too.

When Samson was a young man, he made a promise that he would never cut his hair and he would always follow God. God was happy with Samson and gave him more strength than anyone else alive.

Then one day Samson met a very pretty girl named Delilah. Samson loved Delilah very much.

Did Delilah love Samson too?

Yes. But the Philistines were the enemies of the Israelites. The leaders of the Philistines came to Delilah's house and offered her a lot of money if she would tell them the reason Samson was so strong.

Did Delilah tell them?

She didn't know the reason, but she tried to find out. "Tell me the secret of your great strength," Delilah said to Samson one night.

What did Samson tell her?

Samson told her to tie him up with seven fresh bowstrings—bowstrings so fresh that they had not yet been dried.

Did Delilah try it?

Yes. The Philistines brought her seven fresh bowstrings and then they hid in the house. While Samson was resting, Delilah tied him up with the seven fresh strings.

Then what did Delilah do?

Delilah yelled, "Samson! The Philistines are here!" But Samson just woke up and snapped the strings.

Was Delilah upset?

Yes. "You have made a fool of me," she told Samson, "You lied to me. Tell me the truth now."

"Tie me with new ropes that have never been used," Samson told her.

So did Delilah do that?

Yes. She called the Philistines to hide in her house again. Then, while Samson was resting, she tied him with new ropes.

Did that work?

Delilah thought it would work. "Samson!" Delilah yelled again. "The Philistines are here!"

Samson woke up and snapped the ropes like before.

What did Delilah do then?

She again told Samson he had been making a fool of her and lying to her. She really wanted to know the secret of his strength.

So Samson told her that she should weave the seven braids of his head into a loom and tighten it with a pin.

Did Delilah do that?

Yes. And again, Delilah woke up Samson and yelled, "Samson! The Philistines!"

But Samson just removed the pin and the loom.

What did Delilah do then?

She was very upset. "How can you say you love me when you won't trust me?" she told Samson. Day after day Delilah nagged Samson. Finally, Samson had had enough!

What did Samson tell Delilah?

Samson told Delilah that he had made a promise to God that he would never cut his hair. And if his hair was cut, he would lose all his strength.

So did Delilah cut his hair?

Yes. She called the Philistines to come once more. When Samson fell asleep in her lap, she had a man come in and shave Samson's head.

Again, Delilah woke Samson and said, "Samson! The Philistines!" Samson woke up, not knowing he had lost his strength, and he was captured by the Philistines.

What happened to Samson?

The Philistines put him in their prison and made him do work for them. What they didn't take time to notice was that his hair was growing back.

Then, one day, the Philistines were having a special gathering to honor their god, Dagon. They brought Samson out so they could make fun of him. Samson put his hands on two pillars that held up the building and asked God to give him his strength back one final time.

Then Samson pushed against the pillars and the entire building collapsed, killing Samson and everyone else who was there. So Samson killed more in his death than he had in his life. Samson had learned that only one thing mattered—serving God.

Ruth Believes

Ruth 1:1–4:22

Naomi was married and had two sons. There was a famine, and she and her family moved from Judah to Moab. One day Naomi's husband died. Her two sons grew up and got married. Then her sons died. Now Naomi was alone. The only family she had left were her sons' wives, Orpah and Ruth.

What did Naomi do?

Since there was no one to take care of her and her two daughters-in-law, Naomi thought she would go back home—to Judah.

Did Orpah and Ruth go with her?

Naomi told them to go back to their own homes. She said that they would not find new husbands if they stayed with her.

So what did they do?

Orpah went home.

What about Ruth?

Ruth refused to leave.

"Your people will be my people," Ruth told Naomi, "and your God will be my God."

So did Naomi let Ruth stay with her?

Yes. Naomi could tell that Ruth was not going to leave, so she let Ruth go with her. They traveled from Moab back to Judah. Ruth and Naomi got to Bethlehem. Yes, you're right, the place where Jesus would be born.

Were the people there happy to see Naomi?

Yes. Of course, they did not know Ruth, but they knew Naomi, even though they didn't recognize her at first. Having lost her husband and then her two sons, Naomi looked very sad.

What did Ruth do?

Ruth and Naomi needed food. So Ruth told Naomi she was going out into the fields. After the workers harvested the fields, there was food left over that had not been collected. So Ruth collected it for her and Naomi to eat.

Did she get in trouble for taking food out of someone's field?

The field Ruth was in belonged to Boaz. Boaz was a relative of Naomi. When Boaz saw Ruth in his field, he asked about her and found out she was Naomi's daughter-in-law. He told Ruth that she could continue to glean food from his field.

Did she do that?

Yes, until suppertime. Then Boaz asked Ruth to eat with him and his workers.

Did Ruth's mother-in-law, Naomi, know what happened?

Yes. When Ruth got home, she told Naomi what Boaz had said. Naomi told her that she should stay in Boaz's field because she could be harmed in another field.

Did Ruth do what Naomi said?

Yes. And Boaz asked who it was, just like Naomi said. Ruth said to Boaz, "It is Ruth."

Again, Boaz told Ruth that God would bless her. Soon Ruth and Boaz were married. They had a son, Obed. Obed was the grandfather of King David. And, many years later, another one of Ruth's grandchildren was born—Jesus, the Son of God.

All because Ruth took care of her mother-in-law and did what was right.

Samuel Hears God's Voice

1 Samuel 3:1-21

A woman named Hannah, who was the wife of Elkanah, wanted a baby. She visited the temple every year and prayed that God would give her a baby. "If you will bless me with a baby," she prayed, "I will give him back to you to serve you his entire life."

So shortly after Samuel was born, when he was old enough to live away from his mother, Hannah brought him to the temple. From then on Samuel lived with Eli the priest in the temple.

Then one night something happened that would change the lives of Samuel and Eli forever.

What happened?

Eli had gone to bed, and Samuel also went to bed in the temple area. All the lights were out and Samuel was going to sleep. All of a sudden he heard his name. "Samuel!" the voice called.

What did Samuel do?

Samuel figured it must be Eli calling him for something. After all, Samuel and Eli were the only ones in the temple, so it had to be Eli, right?

"Yes, what do you want?" Samuel asked Eli.

What did Eli say?

"I didn't call you," Eli told Samuel. "Go back to bed."

Did Samuel go back to bed?

Yes. Samuel got back into bed. He was almost asleep when he heard the voice again. "Samuel!" the voice said, just like the first time.

So did Samuel go back to see Eli?

Yes. He figured Eli must want to talk to him. So he walked over to Eli's bedroom.

"What do you want?" Samuel asked Eli. Again.

What did Eli say?

"I did not call you," Eli told Samuel. "Go back and lie down."

So did Samuel go back to bed?

Yes. But as soon as he was in bed, he heard his name being called again.

Did Samuel go to see Eli again?

Yes. Samuel got out of bed and once more walked over to Eli.

What did Eli say?

"I didn't call you," Eli explained again. But Eli thought for a moment. *It must be God calling Samuel*, Eli thought.

"The next time you hear someone calling you," Eli told Samuel, "say, 'Speak, Lord, Your servant is listening.'"

Did Samuel do that?

Yes. He got back into bed. Soon he heard the voice again. "Samuel!"

And Samuel did what Eli told him to do. "Speak, Lord," Samuel said. "Your servant is listening."

What happened then?

The Lord spoke to Samuel. He told Samuel that he wanted him to be the next priest of Israel. God told Samuel exactly what was going to happen and what he wanted Samuel to do.

Samuel became a great spiritual leader in the nation of Israel. All because he listened to God. We have the Bible now with God's words in it. We can listen to God by praying and reading the Bible. Have you listened to God today?

God Feeds Elijah

1 Kings 17:1-24

Elijah was a man of God. He loved God and always tried to obey him. Elijah was also a prophet. A prophet is a messenger of God. A prophet gives the people messages from God and speaks to God for the people. A prophet also knows what is going to happen because God tells him.

King Ahab of Israel was not a good king. He did not love or obey God. One day Elijah had a message for King Ahab.

What was Elijah's message?

Elijah told King Ahab that there would not be rain for the next few years.

What did Elijah do then?

God told Elijah to go and hide by the Kerith Ravine. He could drink from the brook.

What about food?

The ravens fed Elijah. They brought him bread and meat in the morning and in the evening too.

Did the brook run out of water since there was no rain?

Yes, it did. So Elijah went to another place, Zarephath of Sidon. When he got to the town gate at Zarephath, he saw a widow collecting sticks.

What did Elijah say to her?

He asked her to get him some water to drink and a piece of bread. But she said she had no bread. All she had was a little bit of flour and some oil.

Elijah told her to make him some bread and then to make bread for her and her family. "The flour and the oil will not be used up until God sends more rain," Elijah told her.

Did the woman do that?

Yes. This poor woman, with no food or money, believed God and was willing to use the last of her food to help Elijah. She believed God when he told her that her food would last and God took care of her.

She went back home and made the bread. She had plenty of flour and oil to make the bread. It didn't run out, and she was able to continue to make food for Elijah and her family.

Then one day the woman's son became very sick.

Did he get better?

No. He grew worse and worse until he finally died.

What did the woman do?

She went to talk to Elijah. "Why did you do this?" she said to Elijah. "Did you come here to kill my son?"

What did Elijah say?

He told the woman to give him her son.
So Elijah took the woman's son to his
bedroom and laid him on the bed.

What did Elijah do?

Elijah prayed to God and pleaded with him to save
the son. Then Elijah stretched out on top of the boy
and prayed to God again. "O Lord my God, let this
boy's life return to him!" Elijah called out.

Did the boy come alive again?

Yes. Elijah picked up the boy and brought
him to his mother. "Look!" Elijah told her.
"Your son is alive!"

Elijah on Mount Carmel

1 Kings 18:16-39

Elijah had had enough! Do you ever feel that way? Totally frustrated with people who know the right thing to do but won't do it?

That's how Elijah felt. The Israelites wouldn't make a decision. One minute they were following God. The next minute they were following the fake god Baal.

What did Elijah do?

Elijah went to the king of Israel, King Ahab. He told him to set up a meeting for all the people of Israel and the 450 prophets of Baal and the 400 prophets of Asherah.

Who were the prophets of Baal and Asherah?

Baal and Asherah were fake gods made by men. They were poles and statues that people worshipped as if they were living.

Elijah was a prophet because he spoke for God. Baal and Asherah had prophets too. These men spoke for the fake gods Baal and Asherah.

What happened at the meeting?

"It's time to decide," Elijah said. "If Baal is god, follow him. But if the Lord is God, follow him."

What did the people of Israel say?

Nothing. They just stood there and wouldn't say a word!

So then what did Elijah do?

Elijah had an idea. They would prepare a sacrifice for Baal and another sacrifice for God. But the sacrifices would not be put into a fire. They would just be placed on pieces of wood.

Each prophet would pray to his god. The god who set his sacrifice on fire would be the real god.

Everyone thought that was a good idea.

So what happened?

The prophets of Baal prepared their sacrifice first. They put their sacrifice on the wood and began to pray for Baal to set the sacrifice on fire.

Did it work?

What do you think? No, of course not! Elijah then made fun of them, telling them to yell louder. Maybe Baal was out for a walk or he was taking a nap! But nothing happened.

The prophets of Baal yelled to Baal from early in the morning through the evening. But nothing happened.

So what did Elijah do?

First, Elijah repaired the altar of God that had been destroyed. He built a trench around the altar that would hold about 13 quarts of water. Then he cut up the sacrifice and laid it on the pieces of wood.

Then did he pray to God?

Not yet. First Elijah told the men to fill four large jars with water and pour them on the sacrifice and over the wood. Then they did it a second time. And then a third time. The sacrifice and the wood were soaked.

There was so much water there that even the trench was overflowing. It would be hard to set something on fire that was soaked with water, don't you think?

What did Elijah do next?

Elijah prayed. But he didn't pray like many of us pray today. Elijah didn't pray for himself. He prayed that God would show the people that he was the one true God.

How did God answer Elijah's prayer?

God sent a roaring fire down from heaven. It not only burned the sacrifice and the wood, it even burned the ground around the sacrifice where the water had soaked the dirt.

The people of Israel bowed down to the Lord. "The Lord, he is God!" they said. "The Lord, he is God!"

Elijah Runs Away

1 Kings 19:1-18

Elijah was upset. He was also sad, mad, and felt like he didn't have a friend in the world. Elijah was a prophet of God. Elijah's job was to tell people what God wanted them to know and to do. He was to give the people messages from God. Sometimes the messages weren't nice. And sometimes people didn't like hearing what God had to say.

This was one of those times. And the person who was most upset was the queen of Israel, Jezebel.

What did Queen Jezebel say?

She sent a message to Elijah. The message said, "By this time tomorrow I will make sure you are dead."

Wow. What did Elijah do?

What would you do? Yes, he did the same thing. He ran for his life!

Where did Elijah go?

Elijah ran out into the desert. There he found a tree and sat down under it.

"I have had enough, Lord," Elijah said. "Take my life now." Then he went to sleep.

What did God do?

He sent an angel to help Elijah.

The angel tapped Elijah on the shoulder. "Get up and eat," the angel said.

Did Elijah eat?

Elijah sat up and looked around. There was a cake baked over hot coals and a jar of water. So Elijah ate the food and drank the water and went back to sleep.

Did the angel leave?

No, he came back a second time. The angel woke up Elijah again and said, "Get up and eat. The trip is too much for you."

So Elijah ate more food and drank more water. He started walking again.

Where did he go?

Elijah walked for 40 days (more than a month). He finally came to Mount Horeb. Mount Horeb was a special place. It's where Moses talked with God. Elijah found a cave there and spent the night.

God found Elijah in the cave and said, "What are you doing here, Elijah?"

What did Elijah say?

"I have tried so hard, God," Elijah said, "but the people of Israel have rejected you, killed your prophets, and now they are trying to kill me too."

What did God say?

God told Elijah to go out onto the mountain and wait. The Lord was going to pass by him.

What happened?

While Elijah was standing there on the mountain, a big, strong wind came by and shook the mountain.

Was that God?

No, God was not in the wind.

Next, there was an earthquake. The entire mountain shook.

Was that God?

No. God was not in the earth-quake. Next, there was a fire.

Was that God?

No. God was not in the fire. Then Elijah heard a gentle whisper.

Was that God?

Yes! That was God. He told Elijah there were still 7,000 people who were following him. Elijah just needed to keep obeying God and doing what he told him to do.

So when you get discouraged, don't lose heart. Just wait for that gentle whisper from God.

Elijah Goes Home

2 Kings 2:1-15

Think of the person who is most important to you. No, not just a good friend. A person who teaches you how to live your life, is there to give you advice, and helps you know the right thing to do.

How would you feel if suddenly that person left to go home and did not come back? It would be hard, wouldn't it? That's what happened to Elisha.

Who left?

Elijah, who was the prophet of Israel. Elisha was Elijah's helper. Elisha was going to be the next prophet of Israel. Now it was time for Elijah to go up to Heaven. He was going to leave Elisha alone.

Did Elijah leave right away?

No. First Elijah and Elisha had places to go. They walked from Gilgal to Bethel. Then they stopped.

What did they do?

Elijah told Elisha to stay there. He would go to Bethel by himself. Alone.

So did Elisha stay there?

No. "I will not leave you," Elisha told Elijah. So the two prophets walked on to Bethel.

What happened at Bethel?

The prophets at Bethel came up to talk to Elisha.

"Do you know that God is taking Elijah up to Heaven today?" they asked Elisha.

"Yes," Elisha said, "but don't say anything."

So did Elijah and Elisha stay at Bethel?

Elijah told Elisha to stay at Bethel. He was going to go to the city of Jericho.

So did Elisha stay at Bethel?

No. "I will not leave you," he told Elijah again. So the two prophets walked on together to Jericho.

What happened at Jericho?

The prophets at Jericho came out to talk to Elisha. "Do you know that God is bringing Elijah back to Heaven today?" they asked Elisha.

"Yes," Elisha said, "but don't say anything."

No. Elijah told Elisha to stay in Jericho. He was going to the Jordan River.

And, you guessed it, Elisha said, "I will not leave you." So Elijah and Elisha walked on to the Jordan River.

Did they cross the Jordan River?

Yes. Elijah took off his cloak and rolled it up. Then he hit the water with it.

What happened?

The Jordan River divided and Elijah and Elisha walked across to the other side.

What did Elijah say to Elisha then?

He asked Elisha if there was anything he needed before he left. Elisha said he would like a double portion of Elijah's spirit as a prophet of God.

Elijah told Elisha that he was asking a lot. But, if Elisha saw Elijah leaving, then he would have the double portion of his spirit.

Did Elisha see Elijah leaving?

Yes! Just then a chariot of fire and horses of fire came down and Elijah was taken up to Heaven.

"My father! My father! The chariots and horsemen of Israel!" Elisha yelled as Elijah went up to Heaven to be with God.

Did Elisha ever see Elijah again?

No. He picked up Elijah's cloak and struck the Jordan River with it. The water divided, just as it had with Elijah.

The power of being God's prophet was now with Elisha. The job of telling people the messages of God was important.

The Widow's Oil

2 Kings 4:1-7

Have you ever owed anyone money? It's best to not owe people money, isn't it? But sometimes that's hard. A long time ago, if a person couldn't pay back a loan, their children could be taken as slaves to pay back the debt.

That's what happened to this woman whose husband had died.

What did the woman do?

She went to talk to Elisha. Elisha was a prophet. He knew the woman's husband who had died. Elisha knew that her husband loved God. The woman told Elisha that her husband had owed money she could not pay and that the person who loaned him the money was coming to take her sons away as slaves.

What did Elisha say?

Elisha asked the woman what she had in the house.

"There is nothing here at all, except a little oil," she said.

What did Elisha tell her to do?

Elisha told the woman to go to all her neighbors and borrow all the empty jars she could.

What was she supposed to do with the jars?

Elisha told the woman to take the jars into her house and shut and lock the doors behind her and her two sons.

What was the woman to do when she got inside her house?

"Pour oil into all the jars," Elisha told her. "As each jar is filled, put it to one side."

Did the woman run out of oil?

No. The oil kept flowing. The oil did not stop until the last jar was filled.

So what did the woman do then?

The woman went to find Elisha and told him what had happened. She filled up all the jars with the oil.

What did Elisha say?

Elisha told her to go sell the oil and pay back her debts. She was going to be all right, because she trusted God and did what she was told. If we follow God, we will be all right too!

A Room for Elisha

2 Kings 4:8-37

Elisha was a prophet. A prophet was a special person to whom God gave special messages to speak to the people. If people ever wanted to know what to do, they would talk to the prophet, who would then talk to God for them.

One day Elisha went to Shunem. There was a woman there who had a lot of money and a nice home. She wanted to do something special for Elisha.

What did the woman do?

She made a special room for Elisha on her rooftop. Elisha traveled to the town of Shunem a lot. This would give him a room in which to stay whenever he was in town.

So did Elisha stay in the room?

Yes. He liked what the woman did for him. It was very nice. Elisha wanted to do something nice for her too.

What did Elisha do?

Elisha talked with his servant and he
told Elisha that the woman did not
have a son and her husband was old.
So Elisha asked his servant to have
the woman come to talk to him.

What did Elisha tell her?

He told her that next year at this time she would be
holding her new baby boy. The woman did not
believe him.

Did the woman have the baby?

Yes. Just about that same time a year later, the
woman gave birth to a baby boy.

What happened to the woman's son?

He grew up, and one day he was out in the fields working with his father.

"My head! My head!" he complained to his father.

So what did his father do?

He told a servant to take his son to his mother.

What did the woman do when she saw her son?

She held him in her lap until noon, when he died. The woman then laid him on the bed in the room Elisha used and shut the door.

Then what did the woman do?

She called her husband and asked him to get her a donkey and a servant. Then she went to see Elisha.

What did she do when she saw Elisha?

She got off the donkey and knelt down at his feet. "Did I ask you for a son?" she asked Elisha. "Didn't I tell you not to get my hopes up?"

So what did Elisha do?

Elisha called his servant, Gehazi. He gave him his staff and told him to run to the woman's home. When Gehazi got to the home, he placed Elisha's staff over the boy's face.

Did the boy come alive again?

No. So Gehazi ran back to Elisha. He told him that the boy was still dead.

What did Elisha do?

Elisha hurried to the woman's house. He went into the room and shut the door. He then prayed to God for the boy. Then Elisha lay right on top of the boy on the bed. Soon Elisha felt the boy's body become warm. The boy sneezed seven times, and then he opened his eyes.

Did the woman know?

Elisha called her into the room and gave her back her son. The woman trusted God and he took care of her.

David Is Chosen King

1 Samuel 16:1-13

Saul was the first king of Israel. But Saul was not obeying God. He did not love God. God wanted to have a new king—a king who would obey him and love him.

God told Samuel to appoint a new king. Samuel was God's prophet in Israel. God told Samuel what to do, and Samuel told the people what God had said.

Where did God tell Samuel to go to find the new king?

The new king was one of the sons of Jesse. God told Samuel to go to Jesse's house in Bethlehem. God would show Samuel whom he had chosen to be king.

But Samuel was afraid that Saul, the present king, would be mad if he found out what Samuel was doing.

Why would Saul be upset?

Saul wanted to be king. He did not want anyone else to be appointed king. If Saul found out Samuel was going to appoint a new king, he might try to kill Samuel.

137

So what did God tell Samuel to do?

God told Samuel to take an animal with him to see Jesse and his family. Samuel could tell Jesse that he was there to sacrifice to God.

Were the people of Bethlehem happy Samuel was there?

They were afraid. When the elders of the town of Bethlehem saw Samuel, they thought there was something wrong or that Samuel was there to punish them.

"Do you come in peace?" they asked Samuel.

"Yes," Samuel said. "Come to sacrifice with me."

Did he invite Jesse and his family to the sacrifice too?

Yes. He asked Jesse to come and bring all his sons.

Which of Jesse's sons did Samuel see first?

First Samuel saw Eliab. Samuel thought for sure Eliab was the one. But God said, "Do not look at his physical stature. Man looks at the outward appearance, but God looks at the heart."

That's good advice for all of us, isn't it? If we spent as much time on our hearts as we do on how we look, we would be much better followers of God.

Which son did Samuel see next?

Jesse called Abinadab and had him walk in front of Samuel. But Samuel said he wasn't God's choice either.

Then who?

Shammah walked by next, and Samuel said to Jesse, "Nor has the Lord chosen him."

Seven of Jesse's sons walked by Samuel, but none of them were the one God had chosen.

Was that all of Jesse's sons?

That's what Samuel asked Jesse. "Are these all the sons you have?"

"There is one more, my youngest," Jesse told Samuel. "He is out watching the sheep."

Did Samuel want to see him too?

Yes. He told Jesse to go get him. As soon as Samuel saw David, God told him that David was the one. He was to be the next king of Israel.

What did Samuel do?

He anointed David as God's choice, right there in front of everyone. David would be a great king, second only to Jesus.

David and Goliath

1 Samuel 17

A great battle took place one day between the army of Israel and the army of the Philistines. The army of Israel was God's army. But this was not an ordinary battle. The Philistines had a giant on their side. His name was Goliath. He was almost 10 feet tall! Goliath was loud too, and he kept saying mean things to the Israelites and telling them how he would hurt them. For more than a month, the giant yelled and scared the army of Israel.

But the Israelites had God on their side.

Who led Israel's army?

Saul was the king of Israel and the leader of the army. He was a good soldier, and the men of Israel followed him.

There was a man who lived near the battle. The man's name was Jesse. Jesse was getting old. He had eight sons. Jesse's three oldest sons were in the army too. His youngest son was named David. David was too young to fight in the army. David's job was to take care of the family sheep.

Why did David go to the battle?

David's father, Jesse, sent 10 loaves of bread for his sons and the other men in the army. He asked David to take the food to his brothers at the battle.

What did David find when he got there?

David heard Goliath yelling at the army of Israel. It made David angry because he knew God was stronger than any giant, no matter how big the giant was. David talked to King Saul and told him he would fight Goliath.

How would you feel if you were David?

How would you feel facing a 10-foot giant who was yelling that he was going to kill you? Would you be afraid? Would you want to run away for your life?

I would!

How did David feel?

David was angry. David knew God was stronger than any giant. "Who is he to challenge the living God?" David asked.

The next time you face a giant, remember how David felt. God is stronger than anything or anyone.

Why did David want to fight the giant Goliath?

David did not want to fight Goliath for himself. He didn't want to fight Goliath to become popular or to get revenge. David didn't like Goliath's making fun of God. He wanted to prove to Goliath and all the Philistines that David's God, the *real* God, was more powerful than anyone or anything. David wanted to fight Goliath for God!

Did King Saul allow David to fight Goliath?

At first Saul did not want David to fight Goliath. He was just a young boy! But David believed in God. "God will take care of me," David told the king. King Saul agreed to let David fight Goliath. But only if David wore Saul's armor.

The armor was *way* too big for little David! So David went to fight the big giant Goliath with no armor to protect him.

What happened?

Goliath laughed when he saw David come out to fight him. But David didn't care. David knew God would protect him. David had killed a lion and a bear before. He knew God would help him defeat the giant Goliath too.

And God did! David picked up smooth stones in the brook and walked toward Goliath.

"I come to you in the name of the Lord God of Israel," David told him. Just then, David took a stone and shot it toward Goliath. *Smaaackkkk!* The stone hit Goliath right in the middle of the forehead.

Goliath fell forward . . . dead.

How did King Saul reward David?

King Saul was very happy. David had saved Israel. David did not go home after the battle. He stayed with the king in the palace. Saul put David in charge of the men of war. Saul's son, Jonathan, and David became best friends.

Who won the battle against Goliath?

You may think David beat Goliath, but he didn't. God defeated Goliath. David said it best to Goliath, "The battle is the Lord's, and he will deliver you into my hand."

So when you face your next battle, your next difficult homework assignment, your next problem with your friends, your next disagreement with your parents, remember, "The battle is the Lord's."

Wise King Solomon

1 Kings 3:1-28

S olomon was the king of the most powerful nation on Earth—Israel. God told Solomon he would give him anything he wanted. What did Solomon ask God to give him? Wisdom, because he wanted to help people solve their problems. God gave Solomon what he asked for. Solomon was the wisest man who ever lived. People still talk about the wisdom of Solomon. Many people came from all around the world to listen to King Solomon's advice. One day two ladies came to Solomon with a problem.

Who were the women?

The two women lived in the same house. One of the women had a baby. Then, three days later, the other woman had a baby too.

What was the women's problem?

The ladies slept with their babies to keep them safe. One morning when they woke up one of the babies was dead.

How did that happen?

One of the mothers rolled over on top of her baby.

When did she find out her baby was dead?

When the mother woke up in the morning and tried to feed her baby, she looked at her baby and saw that he was dead.

So what did she do?

She was very upset. As she looked at her baby closely, she didn't think he was her baby. She thought he was the other woman's baby.

How could that happen?

The woman told King Solomon that the other mother had rolled on top of her baby during the night. When she realized her baby was dead, the woman gave her dead baby to the other mother and took that woman's live baby.

What did the other woman say?

She was angry! She told King Solomon that what the woman said was a lie. She said that her baby was the live one and the other woman's baby was dead.

So what did King Solomon do?

"Bring me a sword," the king said.

What did he do with the sword?

King Solomon gave this order, "Cut the living child in two and give half to one and half to the other."

What did the mothers say?

One mother said, "Neither of us should have him. Cut him in two!"

But the other mother was very upset. "Please, King Solomon, give her the baby. Don't kill him!"

So what did the king do?

The king gave the baby to the woman who didn't want the baby to be killed. She was willing to give up her baby to save his life. The true sign of the love of a mother. Her child's life was more important than her own happiness. Jesus did the same thing. He gave up his life for ours.

Queen Esther

Esther 2:1–7:10

King Xerxes was upset. He wanted Queen Vashti to entertain his guests at a party. But Queen Vashti did not want to entertain the king's friends. She said no. So Queen Vashti was not allowed to be the queen anymore. King Xerxes would need to find a new queen. He picked Esther. Everyone in the king's palace liked her. But Esther was a Jew. No one knew she was a Jew. She had been brought to Xerxes' kingdom from Israel. And now she was the queen!

Was there a celebration when Esther became queen?

Yes! The king proclaimed the day a special holiday for the new queen. He had a special dinner for her too.

A lot of people were at the city gates talking.

What did they talk about?

Two men were very mad at the king. They were planning to kill him.

Did they do it?

No. Mordecai heard them talking. No one knew it, but Mordecai was Queen Esther's cousin. In fact, Mordecai had raised Esther since her parents had died when she was a little girl. So Mordecai told Esther what he heard, and she told the king.

What did the king do?

The king had the men killed. He was thankful to Mordecai for saving him. What Mordecai did for the king was written in the king's book.

Then King Xerxes promoted Haman. He wanted Haman to be in charge of what happened in the entire kingdom. When Haman walked by, people were expected to bow down to him.

Did everyone bow down to Haman?

Not everyone. Queen Esther's cousin Mordecai refused to bow when Haman walked by him. He told people that he was a Jew and would bow only to God.

What did Haman do?

Haman was very upset at Mordecai. But
Haman didn't want to punish just Mordecai.
He wanted to destroy all the Jews. He went to
the king and asked for permission to destroy
the Jews. Haman didn't know that the queen
was a Jew.

Did the king give him permission?

Yes. So Haman made a rule that all the Jews
would be killed.

Did Mordecai know?

Yes, all the Jews knew. Mordecai was very upset.
He was too upset to go see Esther. So Queen Esther
sent a message to him.

What did Mordecai say?

He told her that Haman was planning to kill all the Jews and she needed to go talk to the king.

Did Esther do that?

No, Esther said that she was allowed to see the king only at certain times. Also, if she told the king that she was a Jew, she might end up getting killed too.

But Mordecai told her that maybe that was the reason she had become queen: to save the Jews.

So what did Queen Esther do?

She told Mordecai that she would go to see the king.

"And if I die, I die," she said.

What did the king say?

The king lifted his special rod to tell Esther is was okay for her to enter and talk to him.

All Esther did was invite King Xerxes and Haman to a special banquet. She told the king there was something she wanted to discuss with him.

What did Haman say?

King Xerxes had been reading in the books of history and found out that Mordecai, Esther's cousin, had never been rewarded for saving the king's life. So he asked Haman to prepare a celebration to honor someone very special.

Haman was very excited. First, the queen invited him to a special banquet. And now, he thought, the king was going to have a celebration just for him. Everything was going so well for Haman, he figured he might as well build a special place to hang Mordecai when he had him killed.

So what happened at the banquet?

Queen Esther told the king that a bad man was wanting to destroy her family.

"Who would do such a terrible thing?" the king asked Esther.

"That terrible man, Haman!" Queen Esther said, pointing her finger at Haman.

So instead of Mordecai dying, King Xerxes put Haman to death. All because Queen Esther believed in God and was brave. Esther thought it was more important to do what God wanted and save her people than to worry about saving herself.

Job

Job 1–2

Job was a special man. And Job loved God very much. Job always tried to obey God and do what would make God happy.

Job had a loving family, great kids, a nice home, and many good things. He was in great health too. But then, one day, that all changed.

What happened?

A messenger came to see Job.

What did the messenger say?

He told Job that his servants who were out taking care of the animals had been attacked, and they were all dead.

What did Job say?

Job didn't have much chance to say anything. The one messenger was barely done talking when another messenger came running up to speak to Job.

What did that messenger say?

He told Job that fire came from the sky and burned up all Job's sheep and the servants who were tending the sheep. They were all dead.

What did Job say?

He didn't have a chance to say anything because another messenger was already talking.

What did that messenger say?

Three bands or raiders took Job's camels and killed his servants who were tending the camels.

Did Job say anything to that messenger?

Again, he didn't have a chance. Another messenger came up to Job right after that. He gave Job terrible news. He said that all Job's children were together eating dinner, and suddenly the house collapsed onto them, and they all died.

So what did Job do?

Of course, Job was very upset. Job tore his clothes and shaved his head. He was very sad. But he did not blame God. Job knew everything he had came from God, so it was okay for God to take it away too.

Then what happened?

Job got sick. He was not going to die, but he was so sick he felt terrible.

Did he get mad at God?

No. His wife told him to get mad at God and die. And Job's friends came over and told him God was punishing him for being bad. But Job knew better. He knew God loved him.

Did Job lose everything?

No. Job stayed true to God. He learned that the only thing that matters is God and making him happy. Job got everything back that he lost—and then some. But, most important, Job learned to trust God.

Daniel Ate His Vegetables

Daniel 1:1-20

The nation of Babylon had taken over the nation of Judah. King Nebuchadnezzar went into Jerusalem and took some of the things out of the temple of God and put them in the temple in Babylon. He also chose the best young men of Judah to become leaders in his kingdom.

Which men did the king choose?

King Nebuchadnezzar wanted only men who were perfect in every way. They would be given special jobs, and he wanted them to do them well.

So the king chose Daniel, Shadrach, Meshach, and Abednego. King Nebuchadnezzar put Ashpenaz, chief of his court officials, in charge of their training. He put them on a special diet too.

What were they supposed to eat?

The men who were being trained to be leaders in the kingdom were to eat the same thing that the king himself ate. King Nebuchadnezzar assigned the amount and type of food.

But Daniel was determined not to eat the king's food. God had told his people not to eat that kind of food.

What did Daniel want to eat?

Daniel, Shadrach, Meshach, and Abednego wanted to eat only vegetables and water. They did not want to eat the meat and the wine and the other kinds of food that the king wanted them to eat.

Daniel asked the chief official, Ashpenaz, if they could follow their own diet of vegetables and water instead.

What did Ashpenaz think?

Ashpenaz was okay with their eating something different from what the king prescribed. But he was worried that Daniel, Shadrach, Meshach, and Abednego would not look as good as the other men and that King Nebuchadnezzar would be upset that they weren't eating the food he wanted them to eat.

What did Daniel say?

Daniel had an idea. "Test us for ten days," he said to the chief official, "and then compare us to the other men who are eating the king's food."

What happened after the ten days?

Daniel, Shadrach, Meshach, and Abednego didn't look like the other men who ate the king's food. They looked better!

So from then on the chief counsel took them off the king's food and let them eat vegetables and drink water instead.

What happened to the four men from Judah?

They spent three years training for for the king's service. After three years the chief counsel took them to King Nebuchadnezzar. They were better than any of the other men, and the king gave them special jobs in the kingdom.

What about Daniel?

God gave Daniel the special ability to understand dreams and foresee the future. Not only was Daniel able to help the king understand his dreams, God also gave Daniel many dreams to explain the future. The book of Daniel contains many such dreams. It is an exciting book!

The Fiery Furnace

Daniel 3:1-30

King Nebuchadnezzar was the king of Babylon. Shadrach, Meshach, and Abednego were Jews from Israel who lived in Babylon. They tried to obey the king and do everything he told them to do. But one day King Nebuchadnezzar asked them to do something they could not do. They had to choose between obeying God and obeying the king.

What did King Nebuchadnezzar do?

The king made a big statue. It was made out of gold and was very tall. The statue was 9 feet wide and 90 feet high, like a nine-story building.

King Nebuchadnezzar then invited all the leaders to come and see the statue.

What did King Nebuchadnezzar want the leaders to do?

The king made an announcement, "When you hear the sound of music playing, you are to bow down to the statue."

Did everyone bow down to the statue?

No. Shadrach, Meshach, and Abednego did not bow to the statue. They bowed only to God.

Did Shadrach, Meshach, and Abednego get in trouble?

Yes. Some people, the Chaldeans, saw Shadrach, Meshach, and Abednego. They saw that they did not bow to the statue. The Chaldeans went to the king and reported to him that the three Jews did not obey his orders.

What did King Nebuchadnezzar say?

The king was very upset. He told Shadrach, Meshach, and Abednego that he wanted to speak with them right away. The king told them that if they did not bow to the statue, they would be thrown into the fiery furnace.

How did Shadrach, Meshach, and Abednego answer him?

They told him that they had to obey God, no matter what punishment the King threatened. "The God we serve is able to deliver us," they told King Nebuchadnezzar, "and even if he doesn't, we will never bow down to your statue."

Did that make King Nebuchadnezzar angry?

Oh, yes. The king was so upset he went into a rage. He ordered that the heat on the furnace be turned up to seven times its normal heat.

What happened to Shadrach, Meshach, and Abednego?

King Nebuchadnezzar ordered that they be bound. When the guards opened the furnace door to put Shadrach, Meshach, and Abednego inside, the heat from the furnace killed the guards immediately.

Did Shadrach, Meshach, and Abednego die too?

No. God sent his angel to keep them safe. King Nebuchadnezzar was amazed. "Didn't we put three men in the furnace?" he asked. "Why do I see four men in there now?"

So what did the king do?

King Nebuchadnezzar had Shadrach, Meshach, and Abednego come out of the furnace. All the leaders of the nation gathered around them. They didn't smell like smoke and no part of them was burned, not even their clothes.

What did King Nebuchadnezzar say to that?

The king had learned who the real God was. He made another announcement. He announced that everyone would follow the one true God from now on. This all came about because Shadrach, Meshach, and Abednego chose to follow God and not the king.

Daniel and the Lions

Daniel 6:1-28

King Darius liked Daniel. In fact the king liked Daniel so much that he was planning to put him in charge of everyone in the kingdom. The other leaders in the kingdom were jealous. They wanted to come up with a plan to get rid of Daniel. They thought and thought and finally came up with a way to trap him that involved Daniel's prayer time with God.

How often did Daniel pray?

Daniel prayed every day. In fact, Daniel prayed to God three times a day, with his windows open.

What was wrong with that? Was praying against the law?

Not at the time. But the leaders who were jealous of Daniel met with the king and talked him into making a new law.

What kind of new law?

The king agreed to a law that would make it illegal for anyone to pray to God. The law required that people pray only to the king and no one else.

Did Daniel stop praying?

No. Daniel knew that the *real* king was God. Daniel believed that the most important thing for him to do was to pray to God. And he kept doing that even though it was against the law. What would you have done?

Did they arrest Daniel?

Of course! The nation's leaders knew exactly what Daniel did every day and when he did it. They were waiting for an opportunity to catch him breaking the law. As soon as Daniel began praying, they were right there to have him arrested and brought before the king.

What did the men tell the king?

The men who had Daniel arrested were quick to remind the king that Daniel had to be thrown in a den of lions because he broke the law. The king felt sad because he liked Daniel. He told Daniel, "May your God rescue you!"

Was Daniel worried?

No. He knew that God would protect him.

Was the king worried?

Yes. He didn't eat or sleep all night.

What happened to Daniel?

God sent an angel to shut the mouths of the lions. Daniel spent the night in the lions' den and wasn't even hurt.

What did the king do?

The king came down to the lions' den first thing the next morning. When he got near the den, the king called out to Daniel, "Daniel, has your God been able to rescue you from the lions?"

What did Daniel say?

He told the king what had happened. King Darius had Daniel lifted out of the lions' den. He then sent out a proclamation that the Lord, the God of Daniel, would be prayed to and followed by everyone in the kingdom, all because Daniel chose to obey God, rather than the king.

Jonah

Jonah 1–4

Would you do whatever God told you to do? Would you go wherever he told you to go? Jonah was a prophet. His job was to give people messages from God. One day God told Jonah to do something special. But Jonah did not want to do it.

What did God want Jonah to do?

God had a message for Nineveh, the capital city of Assyria. The people of Nineveh should stop disobeying God. They should obey God instead.

Why didn't Jonah want to tell the people of Nineveh about God?

The people in the capital of Nineveh, actually the entire nation of Assyria, were the enemies of the nation of Israel. In fact, they were the enemies of God. Jonah did not want to give them a chance to start obeying God. Since the people of Assyria were his enemies, Jonah wanted God to destroy them.

So what did Jonah do?

Jonah needed to take a boat to get to Nineveh, so he walked down to the docks. But instead of getting on the boat to Nineveh, Jonah got on a boat going the opposite direction.

What happened?

Jonah found a quiet place and fell asleep when the boat left the docks. After a little while, the water became very rough. The sailors on the boat were scared.

What did they do?

What do people usually do when they become scared? The sailors prayed.

Did that do any good?

No. Actually, the storm got worse.

Was Jonahd still asleep?

Yes. The captain found Jonah and asked him why he was sleeping when they were in the middle of a storm. Jonah got up and told the men what had happened. He explained that God sent the storm to punish Jonah for disobeying him.

What did Jonah tell them to do?

Jonah told the men to throw him overboard. As soon as the men threw Jonah into the water, the storm stopped and the men were safe.

Did Jonah drown?

No, a great fish swallowed Jonah all in one piece!

Jonah spent three days and three nights inside the fish. And he had a lot of time to think and to pray. He told God he was sorry for disobeying him. And he promised to obey God from then on.

Then what happened?

After three days, the fish threw Jonah up on the land. Jonah was determined to do the right thing then and forever.

So did Jonah ever make it to Nineveh?

Yes. As soon as Jonah had the opportunity, he returned to the docks. But this time he took the right boat—to Nineveh.

He told the people of Nineveh that God loved them, but he was sad that they were not obeying him. Jonah said that they had 40 days to turn back to God and obey him.

The people of Nineveh were very upset. They all promised to obey God from then on. And God forgave them. Jonah learned that God loves everyone and wants us all to follow him.

The New Testament

Jesus Is Born

Luke 2:1-20

Mary was going to have a baby. And she was not married yet. Mary was engaged to be married to Joseph. But Mary's baby was special. Mary's baby was Jesus, God's Son. Jesus would be the Savior of the world.

Did Mary know her baby was special?

Yes. An angel appeared to Mary one day and told her.

Where was Jesus born?

In Bethlehem. Mary and Joseph were from Nazareth.

If they were from Nazareth, why was Jesus born in Bethlehem?

Just before Jesus was born, a census was taken in the Roman Empire. A census is when all the people who live in a certain area are counted.

For this census, everyone had to return to their hometown. And for Mary and Joseph, that was Bethlehem.

Where did Mary and Joseph stay in Bethlehem?

All the inns were full. The only place Mary and Joseph could find to stay was a stable.

So Jesus was born in a stable?

Yes. After his birth, Jesus was placed in a manger with straw.

Was anyone else there?

You mean, besides the animals? There were shepherds there too.

Why were shepherds there?

Earlier that night, angels had visited the shepherds, who were out with their flocks, and told them about Jesus' being born. As soon as the angels left, the shepherds decided they wanted to see Jesus too. So they went to Bethlehem and found Mary and Joseph and Jesus in the stable.

What did Mary think of all this?

It was a very special time for her. She remembered everything that was happening, and later on, she thought about what everyone said about Jesus.

The Angel's Announcement

Luke 2:8-16

Angels are God's messengers. God created them and gives them jobs to do. Sometimes angels are sent to protect people. And sometimes they are sent to give messages from God. The most important message angels have ever had to give was when Jesus was born.

Who did the angel give the message to?

If you had the best message in the history of the world that you wanted everyone to hear, who would you announce it to? Probably someone very important, right? Someone who could get the word out to others. Someone everyone respected. But that's not what this angel did. The angel gave the message to a group of shepherds.

Shepherds? You mean the men watching the sheep?

Yes. They would be common workers today. The people doing the hard work—the ones who do things like fix the roads, clean the offices, cut the grass, and sweep the floors.

God chose these people to hear this great message. The message that Jesus, God's Son, the Savior of the world, had been born.

But why the shepherds? Why not the king or other world leaders?

Because Jesus came for the regular people. Jesus cared about every person in every town, not just the rich and the famous. Jesus came for everyone.

Jesus doesn't care how important a person is. He loves every one of us. You are special to God, and he cares about everything you do.

When did the angel speak to the shepherds?

It was at night. The shepherds were out in the fields with their sheep, and no one else was around.

Weren't the shepherds scared?

Yes, they were terrified. Here they were, in the middle of the night, in an empty field. And an angel showed up in front of them. They didn't hear him coming or see him in the distance. He just appeared with no warning.

How could they see the angel? Wasn't it dark?

You don't miss an angel. The Bible says that the glory of God was all around the shepherds. The entire sky was bright, like it was the middle of the day.

What did the angel say to them?

He told them not to be afraid. Jesus, the Savior, had been born.

God wants to give us good news. He loves us and wants us to trust him. We shouldn't be afraid when God has something to tell us.

Then what happened?

The Bible tells us that a *multitude* of angels joined the one angel. We don't really know how many angels there were. Probably more than the shepherds could count.

And what did all these angels say?

"Glory to God in the highest, and on earth, peace and goodwill toward men."

It was like a worship service in the middle of the night.

What did the shepherds do then?

What would you do? They ran as fast as they could to Bethlehem. That's where the angels said Jesus had been born.

Did they find Jesus?

Yes, exactly as the angel had described. The angel had said that Jesus would be wrapped up in cloths and lying in a manger. And that's where they found him, with Mary and Joseph.

The shepherds then spread the news to everyone about what the angels told them and how they saw Jesus. They were the first ones to tell the Christmas story!

The Wise Men Visit Jesus

Matthew 2:1-20

Men who study the stars are always looking for stars that are different. One night some wise men saw a star that they had never seen before and would never see again.

So what did the wise men do?

They got on their camels and began to follow the bright star.

Where did they go?

They followed the star as far as Jerusalem. When they arrived in Jerusalem, the wise men asked where the King of the Jews was to be born.

King Herod heard about the wise men. He was very upset when he heard that a king of the Jews was born. In fact, everyone in Jerusalem was upset.

So what did King Herod do?

He set up a meeting with the teachers and leaders of the Jews. "Where is the King of the Jews to be born?" Herod asked them.

"In Bethlehem," they answered him.

So what did Herod do then?

He met with the wise men. Herod didn't want anyone to know he was meeting with them, so he held the meeting in secret. He asked them when they first saw the star and told them to let him know when they found the baby, the new King of the Jews.

Did the wise men find Jesus?

Yes. They kept following the star, and one day the star stopped right above a house.

Did the wise men go into the house?

Yes. They saw Jesus and worshipped him. Remember, they had been looking for Jesus for a long time ever since Jesus had been born. No, Jesus was not still in the manger. The wise men found Jesus long after that.

What did they do when they saw Jesus?

They had brought gifts for him since he was the King of kings. People were expected to give gifts to a new king.

So the wise men gave gifts of gold, frankincense, and myrrh.

Did they tell Herod they found Jesus?

No. All Herod wanted to do was to hurt Jesus. So God warned the wise men in a dream not to go back to Herod. They followed another route home so they did not see Herod.

Did God warn Mary and Joseph too?

Yes. God told Mary's husband, Joseph, to flee to Egypt with Mary and Jesus.

Why did they move to Egypt?

Because Herod found out that the wise men had tricked him, and he was going to hurt all the babies who were born about the same time that Jesus was born. Herod did not like it that someone else might replace him as king.

God kept Jesus safe so that Jesus could save us from our sins.

Young Jesus at the Temple

Luke 2:41-51

Jerusalem was a special place. It was where the Jews, God's chosen people, went to worship him. Jerusalem was also where King David's palace was and where Solomon built a temple to worship God. Jerusalem was the capital of Israel. It was *the* place to be for the Jews. Every spring, Jesus' parents, Mary and Joseph, traveled to Jerusalem to worship God.

Why did they go at this time of year?

For the Feast of Passover. The Passover was a very important time when the Jews remembered how God rescued them from slavery in Egypt and brought them to the land of Israel. You can read about the first Passover in Exodus 12, 13.

Did Jesus and his parents go to Jerusalem alone?

No. Many, many people went to Jerusalem for the Passover. Jesus and his parents traveled in a long caravan of family and friends.

How long was the trip?

It took several days to travel from Nazareth, Jesus' hometown, to Jerusalem. When they arrived in Jerusalem, Jesus and his parents spent the week celebrating Passover in Jerusalem with the other Jews.

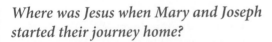

Did they travel home then?

Yes. After the Passover week, Mary and Joseph traveled back hoome together with their friends and relatives.

Where was Jesus when Mary and Joseph started their journey home?

Jesus was back in the temple in Jerusalem, talking to the teachers and leaders. He was asking them questions about Scripture. Jesus was 12 years old. The teachers and leaders in the temple with very impressed with Jesus' questions and knowledge of Scripture.

Did Mary and Joseph know Jesus was back in the temple in Jerusalem?

No, they thought Jesus was with someone else in the group traveling back home. There were many people traveling together in the caravan. Jesus could easily have been traveling with another family in the group.

What did they do?

Once Mary and Joseph found out Jesus wasn't with them, they went back through the group of people in the caravan to see if Jesus was with another family or if anyone had seen him.

Did they find Jesus?

No. Mary and Joseph ended up traveling all the way back to Jerusalem. Even when they returned to the city, they didn't find Jesus right away. It took them three days of searching throughout Jerusalem before they found Jesus in the temple.

Mary was very upset. "Why have you treated us this way?" she asked Jesus. "Your father and I have been looking everywhere for you!"

What did Jesus say?

"Why were you looking for me?" Jesus asked his mother. "Didn't you know I had to be in my Father's house?"

What did Jesus mean by that?

He meant he needed to be in the temple talking about God. Mary and Joseph didn't understand him either. But later on, Mary remembered what had happened and what Jesus had said. It made sense to them. Jesus' answer is good advice for all of us. We need to spend time in God's house doing God's work.

Jesus Is Baptized

Matthew 3:1-17

Do you have a best friend? Someone who "has your back"? John the Baptist was that kind of friend for Jesus. Actually, John and Jesus were cousins. John the Baptist's job was to introduce Jesus to the world.

How did John the Baptist introduce Jesus?

John, who lived out in the desert and ate honey and bugs for food, told everyone he met that Jesus was coming.

What did John say?

John told people to get ready because Jesus was coming soon. He said that Jesus would punish people who were disobeying God. John said that he wasn't good enough to even tie Jesus' sandals.

He told the people to do the same thing we should all do. Tell God we're sorry for our sins and ask him to forgive us.

Did they do that? Did they tell God they were sorry?

Not everyone. Some did, and John baptized them. But others didn't like what John was telling them. They didn't like hearing that they were sinners and had disobeyed God.

What did they say to John?

They wanted to know who John was and what right he had to be saying these things and telling them that they needed to get right with God.

How did John respond?

He told them he was not Jesus but was sent to prepare the way for Jesus and tell people to get ready. The people knew what John meant because God had told them long ago that a man would appear out of the wilderness saying, "Make straight the way of the Lord."

So what did John do when he saw Jesus coming?

He said, "Behold, the Lamb of God who takes away the sin of the world." Jesus told John that he was there to be baptized.

Did John baptize Jesus right away?

No. John didn't understand why Jesus needed to be baptized. Baptism was for people who had been disobeying God. Jesus was the Son of God. He didn't need to be baptized.

How did Jesus convince him?

"Let it be so," Jesus said to John, "so that we do what should be done." Jesus wanted to be baptized as an example to others in the world at that time and to us too.

Did John baptize Jesus then?

Yes. Jesus and John went into the water, and John baptized him.

Then what happened?

As soon as Jesus was baptized and he came out of the water, a dove appeared from heaven and a voice said, "This is my beloved Son, in whom I am well pleased."

Who was speaking?

God. Jesus was God's Son, and he wanted everyone to know that. And the dove was the Holy Spirit. He flew and rested on Jesus as he came out of the water. Jesus was very special, and God wanted everyone to know him. We need to make sure all our friends know about Jesus too.

Jesus Is Tempted

Luke 4:1-13

Have you ever done anything wrong? What or who made you do it? It's normal to think about doing something wrong. Sometimes you are tempted to do wrong by someone or something. Even Jesus was tempted to do wrong.

When was Jesus ever tempted to do wrong?

It happened right after Jesus was batized. That's the way it usually goes, isn't it? Right at the moment we have a great experience and feel close to God is when we are tempted to disobey God and do something wrong.

The Spirit of God led Jesus out into the wilderness and left him all alone.

How could Jesus eat in the wilderness?

He didn't. He was in the wilderness for 40 days and didn't eat anything.

Didn't Jesus get hungry?

Yes. Jesus was very hungry. You would be hungry too, if you hadn't eaten for more than a month.

What happened to Jesus?

Satan thought Jesus' being hungry would be a way to get him to sin, to disobey God. He said to Jesus, "If You are the Son of God, tell this stone to become bread."

Did Jesus do it?

No. Jesus quoted Deuteronomy 8:3 to Satan. He said, "Man does not live by bread alone." The best way to defeat Satan and not give in to temptation is to use the Bible, God's Word.

What did Satan do then?

He took Jesus up to a high place and showed him all the kingdoms of the world. Remember that Satan was called "the prince of the world." He offered to give the world to Jesus. All Jesus had to do was worship him.

Did Jesus do it?

No. Jesus reminded Satan about the commandment in Deuteronomy 6:13 that says, "Worship the Lord your God and serve him only."

Did Satan give up then?

No. He made one more try at tempting Jesus. This time Satan quoted Psalm 91:11, 12 to Jesus in an attempt to get him to sin. He took Jesus to the highest point of the temple and told him to jump! Satan twisted God's words to try to get Jesus to do wrong.

"The Bible says," Satan reminded Jesus, "that he will command his angels concerning you to guard you carefully; they will lift you up in their hands, so that you will not strike your foot against a stone."

What did Jesus say to that?

Jesus quoted Deuteronomy 6:16. "Do not put the Lord your God to the test," Jesus told Satan.

Jesus was always one step ahead of Satan. If you want to defeat Satan when he tempts you to do wrong, ask Jesus for help. He knows how to win!

Jesus Clears the Temple

John 2:12-23

The temple was a special place. It was like a church building is today. It was the place people came to pray to God. Passover was the time of the year when the Jewish people remembered how God saved them from slavery in Egypt and how Moses led them through the wilderness to the Promised Land.

Jesus went into the temple to worship at Passover and he became very upset.

What made Jesus so angry?

Jesus went into the temple to pray and worship God. Inside the gates of the temple was a large courtyard. The courtyard was filled with men selling animals and other things. It was like a regular marketplace.

Why were they selling animals?

People came into the temple, especially during Passover, to make sacrifices to God. If they didn't bring animals with them to sacrifice, they would buy the animals when they arrived at the temple before they went in to sacrifice.

What was wrong with that?

It was wrong because it was done in the temple, in the house of God. This was a special place, a place people came to talk to God.

So what did Jesus do?

He took several cords of rope and twisted them together to make a strong whip.

What did Jesus do with the whip?

He forced everyone who was selling to leave with their animals. Jesus even turned over the tables. Money was flying everywhere, all over the courtyard.

Did Jesus say anything to the sellers?

Yes. He said, "Get these out of here! How dare you turn my Father's house into a market!"

Didn't anyone object to what Jesus was doing?

Yes. The Jewish leaders did. They said, "What gives you the authority to do all this? What sign are you going to perform?"

So did Jesus give them a sign?

Yes, in a way. He told them to destroy the temple, and he would rebuild it in three days.

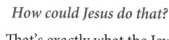

How could Jesus do that?

That's exactly what the Jewish leaders asked. They told Jesus it took them 46 years to build the temple. They didn't understand how he could rebuild it in three days!

So what did Jesus mean?

He was talking about the temple of his body. After Jesus died for our sins on the cross, he rose from the dead three days later. When Jesus was resurrected, the disciples remembered what he told the Jews at the temple.

So did the leaders at the temple believe Jesus?

No. Not then, anyway. But during the Passover Festival in Jerusalem, Jesus performed many miracles, and many of the people there believed in him.

Jesus Calls His Disciples

Luke 5:1-11

Jesus was a teacher. Most people call him the great teacher. A great teacher needs great students. So Jesus was choosing men to be his disciples. They would learn much from Jesus, and then they would spend their lives telling people what they had learned.

How did Jesus find his disciples?

One day Jesus was teaching people by the shore. It was very crowded.

So what did Jesus do?

Jesus saw some boats and got in one of them.

Whose boat was it?

The boat belonged to Peter. Jesus asked Peter to push the boat out from the shore. Jesus then got in the boat and taught the people who were gathered together on the shore.

What did Jesus do when he was finished teaching?

He told Peter to take the boat out to the deep waters and let down the nets into the water.

Did Peter do that?

Yes. Peter said, "We've worked hard all night and haven't caught anything. But because you say so, I will let down the nets."

Did Peter catch anything?

Oh, yes. He caught so much he had to get help from another fishing boat. And the two boats were soon filled with fish.

What did Peter think?

He was scared. He bowed down before Jesus and said that Jesus should get away from him. Peter didn't think he was good enough to be with Jesus.

What did Jesus say?

"Don't be afraid," Jesus told Peter. "From now on you will catch men."

Jesus Saves the Wedding

John 2:1-11

Everyone was excited! A wedding was being held in Cana, in Galilee. It was a happy day and everyone was there, including Jesus' mother.

Was Jesus there?

Yes. Jesus and his disciples were at the wedding too.

What happened at the wedding?

There was a lot of wine to drink and everyone was having a lot of fun. But then the wine ran out.

How were they going to get more wine?

Jesus' mother went to find Jesus. "They are out of wine," she said.

What did Jesus say?

"Why are you telling me this?" Jesus asked his mother.

What did his mother say?

She didn't say anything to Jesus. She turned to the servants there at the wedding and said, "Do whatever he tells you."

So what did Jesus tell the servants to do?

There were six big stone jars nearby. Jesus told the servants to fill the jars to the top with water.

Then what?

When the jars were filled with water, Jesus told the servants to take some wine to the head of the reception and let him try it.

What did he say?

He called the groom over and told him this was the best wine he had served during the entire wedding.

This was the first of many things Jesus would do to help people and to show he was God's Son. Jesus controls many things, even wine at a wedding. Don't you think he can fix your problems too?

Jesus Heals the Paralyzed Man

Mark 2:1-12

Jesus was very popular. Everyone wanted to see him and listen to what he had to say. Many people brought their sick friends and members of their families to Jesus so that he could heal them.

One day Jesus came to the town of Capernaum to visit his friends. He stayed with one of his friends overnight. But soon word got out that Jesus was in town.

What happened?

As soon as people found out where Jesus was staying, they all came over to see him.

Wasn't the house crowded?

It was so crowded that people were waiting outside the house trying to get in or at least listen to Jesus. One man wanted to get in to see Jesus, but he couldn't walk because he was paralyzed.

How did he get to the house where Jesus was staying?

He lay on a mat and four of his friends carried him.

Did they get in to see Jesus?

No, it was so crowded that there wasn't even room for people to stand outside and listen to Jesus.

So what did they do?

The men carried their friend on the mat up to the roof.

What did they do on the roof?

The men removed some roof tiles and dug an opening into the roof.

Then what did they do?

The men lowered the paralyzed man on his mat down into the home right in front of Jesus.

What was Jesus' reaction?

After seeing all their work just to get their friend in front of him, Jesus was very impressed with their faith.

He turned to the man on the mat and said, "Son, your sins are forgiven."

Were the people surprised?

Yes. There were Jewish leaders there, and they thought it was wrong for Jesus to tell the man his sins were forgiven. Only God can forgive sins. They were mad that Jesus told the man his sins were forgiven. Jesus knows everything, so he knew what the Jewish leaders were thinking.

What did Jesus say?

He said to them, "Why are you thinking these things? Which is easier? To say 'Your sins are forgiven'? or to say, 'Get up, take your mat and walk?' I am the Son of Man and I have the power on earth to forgive sins."

Jesus then turned to the man and said, "I tell you, get up, take your mat, and go home!"

Did the man get up?

Yes! Right away the man got up, picked up his mat, and walked out of the house. Everyone was amazed.

"We have never seen anything like this," the people said. The paralyzed man was healed, all because he and his four friends had faith and believed that Jesus could help them.

The Prodigal Son

Luke 15:11-32

Jesus loved telling stories. All of Jesus' stories had a point to them. Jesus always taught something very important in his stories.

One day Jesus was trying to explain how much God loves everyone, so he told the story of a man with two sons. One day the youngest son wanted his share of his inheritance. He wanted the money now instead of waiting until after his father died.

What did his father say?

The father agreed and divided the inheritance among his two sons. He gave each of them half of everything he had.

So what did the youngest son do?

A short time after he received his inheritance, he packed all his things and left.

Where did he go?

He traveled to a country far away.

What did he do there?

He had the time of his life. He went to every party he could attend. He lived it up. Soon, all his money was gone.

How did he survive without any money?

He got a job feeding the pigs. The young son was so hungry, he would have loved to eat the pigs' food.

Finally, it dawned on him. His father's servants lived better than he did . He would return to his father and ask to be one of his workers.

So did he go back home?

Yes. The son traveled all the way back home to his father's house.

What did his father do?

When his father saw him coming from a long way away, he ran out to meet him. He was so excited his son was home. He asked his servants to prepare a big feast and have a party for his son.

Where was the other son, the older one?

He was out in the fields working. He asked one of the other workers what was going on. The worker told him that his younger brother had come home and his father was throwing a big party for him.

Did the older brother go to the party?

No, he refused.

Did his father know he was outside?

Yes. His father came out to ask him to come in to the party.

"I have been working for you all these years and never disobeyed you and never asked for a thing," his oldest son complained, "but when your son comes home after wasting all his money, you throw him a party."

"You are always with me, my son, and everything I have is yours," the father answered him, "but we have to celebrate and be glad because your brother was dead and now is alive. He was lost and now he's found."

Why did Jesus tell this story?

Jesus wanted everyone to know how much God loves us and that God doesn't play favorites. He loves everyone the same. God is still waiting for even people who live bad lives to come back to him. You can always come back to God, and he will always welcome you home!

The Good Samaritan

Luke 10:25-37

Who are your friends? Are you nice to just your friends or to everyone? Jesus said we are to love our neighbors.

Who is my neighbor?

That's exactly what Jesus was asked. Many times Jesus answered questions with more questions. Other times he answered questions by telling stories.

That's what Jesus did when he was asked about our neighbors. He told the story about the good Samaritan. Have you ever heard someone called a good Samaritan? Well, the term "Good Samaritan" comes from this story Jesus told.

What is a Samaritan?

When the nation of Israel was defeated and the Jews were taken into captivity as slaves, some of the Jews were left behind. Many of the people from Assyria came into Israel and married the Jewish people. As a result, they had children who were part Jewish and part non-Jewish. These children were called Samaritans. The Jews never accepted the Samaritans. They didn't think they were real Jews.

So Jesus told this story about the Samaritans?

Actually, the story begins with another man walking along the road. Suddenly a group of robbers attacked him, beat him up, and took all his money.

Did they kill him?

Not quite. But he was very badly beaten and the robbers had taken all his clothes. If someone hadn't helped him soon, he probably would have died.

Weren't there other people around to help him?

No, not at that time. There was no one there when he was beaten. And it was a while before anyone came down the road. Eventually, though, a man appeared. A priest. The priests were the religious leaders. They were the people who helped the Jews learn about and obey God.

He helped the poor man, right?

No, not only did the priest not help the man, he crossed the road and walked on the other side so he wouldn't have to walk by the man who'd been beaten.

Did someone else come by?

Yes, later a Levite walked down the road. A Levite was a person who was a member of the tribe of Levi. People in Levi's family assisted the priests.

Did he help the man?

No, he also crossed over to the other side of the road and walked right by so he didn't have to look at the man who was hurt.

That's awful! Did the man ever get any help?

Yes. Finally, another man walked on the road. He was a Samaritan, of all people! He stopped, looked at the man, and felt sorry for him.

So what did the Samaritan do?

First, he bandaged up the man's wounds. He poured oil and wine on them to help heal them. Remember, the man had been beaten and left naked on the side of the road, so he was in bad shape.

Then the Samaritan put the man on his own donkey and took him to a hotel.

Did he leave him there?

He spent the night taking care of him at the hotel. The next day he gave money to the hotel manager and asked him to take care of him.

The Samaritan told the manager that if the man's care cost any more money than that, he would pay him when he returned.

After telling the story, Jesus asked, "Who do you think was a neighbor to the man?"

What did the people say?

They gave the right answer, "The man who helped him." And Jesus then told them, "Go and do likewise."

We should be nice to everyone, not just our friends.

Jesus Heals Ten Lepers

Luke 17:11-19

Have you ever done something nice for someone? What did the person say? Hopefully she said, "Thank you."

One day Jesus and his disciples were walking to Jerusalem from Galilee. They had to go through Samaria to get to Jerusalem, which was in Judea, just South of Samaria.

As Jesus and his disciples were walking, they saw a group of ten men standing far away from other people. These men were lepers.

What is a leper?

A leper is a person with leprosy. Leprosy is a terrible disease. It was like a death sentence in Bible times. Once a person had leprosy, he spent a sad, lonely life waiting to die.

Why were they lonely?

Because other people were scared they might catch leprosy too, and die. Lepers were not allowed to talk to people without leprosy. They were forced to live far away from everyone else.

Did the lepers talk to Jesus?

They stayed a distance away from Jesus when they saw him. Then they yelled loudly, "Jesus! Master! Help us!"

Did Jesus heal them?

Yes. All he said was, "Go, show yourselves to the priests."

What happened then?

As they went to see the priests, they were healed and their leprosy was gone.

Why did they have to go to the priest?

They had to show themselves to the priests so the priests could declare them clean and free of any leprosy. Then they could return to their families and to their lives. They could be around other people again.

Did anyone say thank you to Jesus?

One man did. As soon as he was healed, he
came back to Jesus, yelling very loudly and
giving thanks to God. He got down on his
knees and thanked Jesus. The man was a
Samaritan.

What did Jesus say?

"Weren't ten men healed?" Jesus asked.
"Where are the other nine? Only this for-
eigner came back to give thanks to God?" Remember, the Samaritan was the only one who
returned to thank Jesus for healing him. But
God doesn't care. Jesus' love is for everyone.

What did Jesus tell the man to do?

He told him to get up and go. "Your faith has
made you well," Jesus said.

Even today, Jesus wants us to show we have faith
and take the first steps to obey him, just as the
10 lepers did.

Jesus Has a Visitor— Nicodemus

John 3:1-21

Jesus had a lot of friends. He was a great teacher, and people loved hearing him. Jesus taught people about God. He helped them to live the right way.

One night a religious leader of the Jews came to talk to Jesus. This man's name was Nicodemus.

Who were the religious leaders?

The religious leaders were called Pharisees. They taught the Jewish people about God. They also created rules about how to live for God.

Nicodemus was one of them.

Did Nicodemus like Jesus too?

Nicodemus liked Jesus. But most of the Pharisees didn't like Jesus. They didn't like how Jesus told the people that the Pharisees' rules were wrong.

Were the Pharisees mad at Nicodemus for going to talk to Jesus?

Yes, that's why Nicodemus went to see Jesus at night, when it was dark. He didn't want the Pharisees to know he was talking to Jesus.

But we need to let our friends know we love Jesus. We shouldn't hide our love for him. We should talk to Jesus during the day when everyone can see us.

What did Nicodemus say to Jesus?

Nicodemus told Jesus that he knew Jesus was from God because of all the good things Jesus did, the miracles he performed, and the way he healed people.

What did Jesus say?

Jesus told Nicodemus that he needed to be born again. Nicodemus didn't understand what Jesus meant. He asked Jesus, "How can a person be born a second time?"

What did Jesus mean?

Jesus explained that Nicodemus needed to be born of the Spirit. When we are born again God will help us obey him. Jesus told Nicodemus, "What is born of the Spirit is spirit."

Did Nicodemus understand that?

Nicodemus did not understand what Jesus was saying. So Jesus explained that whoever believes in him would not perish but would have eternal life.

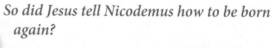

So did Jesus tell Nicodemus how to be born again?

Since Nicodemus was a Jewish religious leader, he knew all about Moses. Jesus reminded Nicodemus about the time when Moses raised the serpent in the wilderness. Everyone who looked at the serpent would live. You can read about that in Numbers 21.

So what does that have to do with being born again?

Jesus said, "Just as Moses raised the serpent in the wilderness, so must the Son of Man be lifted up." He was talking about his death on the cross. And, just like with the serpent in the wilderness, those who believe in Jesus and his death on the cross will be born again and will live.

Is that what John 3:16 says?

Yes, actually, John 3:16 is part of Jesus' conversation with Nicodemus. We often think of that verse by itself, but it was the most important thing Jesus had to tell Nicodemus. "For God so loved the world, that he gave his only begotten Son, that whosoever believes in him shall not perish, but have everlasting life."

Jesus Stops a Storm

Mark 4:35-41

Have you ever been on a boat during a storm? Were you scared? What happened? One day Jesus' disciples were on a boat in the middle of a storm. They were scared too.

What happened?

The disciples were fishermen. They had spent many hours in boats out on the water. But this storm was different. The boat was shaking, and they thought it might tip over.

What did the disciples do?

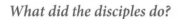

The disciples did what every fisherman would do. They did everything they could to steady the boat. They grabbed buckets and tried to get the water out of the boat. They were fighting for their lives.

Was Jesus on the boat too?

Yes, Jesus was on the boat with the disciples. He was in the back of the boat. He was asleep.

Did the disciples wake Jesus?

Yes, of course. They couldn't believe Jesus was sleeping during such a bad storm.

What did they say to Jesus?

The disciples were really scared now. "Don't you care that we are all dying?" they yelled at Jesus.

What did Jesus do?

He turned to face the wind and the waves and said, "Hush! Be still!"

Did that help?

Yes! Right away, the storm stopped and the water became calm again. Remember, Jesus is God's Son. The Bible tells us that he created the world. So, of course the wind would do what he told it to do. He created the wind.

What did the disciples think when the storm calmed?

They were afraid.

Did Jesus say anything to them?

Yes. He asked, "Why are you so scared? Why do you not have any faith?" Jesus was with them on the boat. He had been teaching them that God would take care of them, even during a storm. God will take care of you too. You just need to trust him.

What did the disciples say?

They were still scared and amazed at what had happened. "Who is this?" they said to one another, "that even the wind and the sea obey him?"

Jesus Helps Jairus's Daughter

Mark 5:21-43

Jesus loved helping people. He especially loved healing the sick. But most of all, Jesus loved helping people follow God. So everywhere Jesus went, many people followed. One day the leader of the synagogue, Jairus, needed Jesus' help.

What did Jairus ask Jesus?

As soon as he saw Jesus, he bowed down in front of him. "My little girl is dying," Jairus said to Jesus. "Please come and heal her."

Were there a lot of other people who wanted to see Jesus?

Yes. There was a large crowd all around Jesus. One woman wanted to try to touch Jesus' cloak. She thought that she would be healed if she could only touch his cloak.

Was she able to touch Jesus' cloak?

Yes. She was able to touch his cloak. And as soon as she did, she was healed.

Did Jesus agree to go see Jairus's daughter?

Yes. Jesus and Jarius were on their way to see the little girl when some men came from Jairus's house. "Your daughter is dead," they told Jairus. "Don't bother Jesus anymore."

What did Jesus say?

Jesus turned to Jairus and said, "Don't be afraid—just believe."

Did everyone follow Jesus to Jairus's house?

No. Only Peter, James, and John went with Jesus to Jairus' house.

What was going on at Jairus's home?

There were people everywhere. They were all crying. Jairus's daughter was only 12 years old. Jesus told them that the child was not dead, she was just asleep. But they all just laughed at him.

What did Jesus do?

Jesus told everyone to leave, and he went into the child's room with her parents and Peter, James, and John.

Did Jesus say or do anything to the child?

Yes. He took her hand and said, "Little girl, get up!"

And did she?

Yes! Right away she sat up and started walking around the house. Jesus was right when he told Jairus, "Don't be afraid; just believe."

If we believe Jesus, he will take care of us too.

Jesus Feeds 5,000

Matthew 14:13-21

Jesus was very popular because he was healing so many people who were sick. Wherever Jesus went with his disciples, people followed him. They wanted to hear what Jesus had to say and ask him questions. And they also wanted him to heal them.

One day Jesus and his disciples traveled in a boat to the other side of the Sea of Galilee, away from the city.

Did the people follow them?

Yes. As soon as they saw Jesus and his disciples get in the boat to cross over to the other side of the sea, the people began to walk around the water to meet them on the other side.

How many people were there?

The Bible says there were 5,000 men. But that count doesn't include the women and children. Some people believe there were as many as 15,000 people there with Jesus.

Where was Jesus?

Jesus was up on the mountain on the other side of the Sea of Galilee. He was sitting with his disciples and teaching them.

Did Jesus know that all the people were there?

Yes. After he spoke with the disciples, Jesus came down from the mountain and saw all the people.

What did Jesus do?

Jesus felt sorry for them when he saw them. So he taught them about God. Many of the people were sick or with sick people, and Jesus healed them.

How long were they there with Jesus?

Into the evening. The disciples wanted Jesus to let the people go home so they could get something to eat.

"This place is in the middle of nowhere," the disciples told Jesus. "Send the people away so that they can go buy food for themselves."

Did Jesus send them home?

No. He told the disciples that the people didn't need to leave. "Give them something to eat," Jesus said.

What did the disciples think about feeding the crowd?

One of the disciples, Philip, told Jesus that it would cost almost as much money as a person earned in a year to buy enough food to feed all those people.

Another one of the disciples, Andrew, told Jesus that a boy was there who had five loaves of bread and two fish with him.

Did Jesus take the boy's food?

Yes. Jesus told Andrew to bring the food to him and to tell everyone to sit down on the grass. He then prayed for the food and gave thanks to God for providing it. Do you and your family thank God for your food too?

Was there enough food for everyone?

Yes, there was more than enough food for the thousands of people who were there that day. Everyone had as much as they wanted, and then Jesus told the disciples to collect all the leftovers. There was enough food remaining to fill 12 baskets!

God knew what the people needed, and he provided more than enough to satisfy them. He does the same for us today if we trust him.

Jesus Walks on Water

Matthew 14:22-33

Jesus had been teaching all day. He was tired, and he wanted to spend time praying to God. So Jesus told the disciples to take the boat to the other side of the lake and he would walk over and meet them there.

What did Jesus do then?

Jesus went up on the mountain to pray. Jesus spent a lot of time praying. That's a good example for all of us.

Did the disciples take the boat to the other side?

They started to take the boat out. They got partway out on the water and it began to get dark.

Then what happened?

When it got dark the waves became rough. The disciples were working hard to keep the boat afloat. It was being tossed back and forth on the water.

Were the disciples getting scared?

Yes. It was the middle of the night. Then they looked up and saw a man walking toward them.

They thought they were seeing things or that it was a ghost.

What was it?

It was Jesus. "Be not afraid," Jesus told them. "It is I."

What did the disciples say?

Peter yelled out, "If it is you, Lord, tell me to come out onto the water."

Did Jesus tell him to come out on the water?

Yes. "Come," Jesus said. So Peter got out of the boat.

Did Peter walk on the water too?

Yes. He was walking right toward Jesus.

Then what happened?

Peter saw all the waves. Remember, they were in the middle of a storm. He became afraid, and he began sinking.

So what did Peter do?

He reached out his hand to Jesus.

"Save me, Lord!" Peter yelled.

So did Jesus save him?

Yes. Jesus took Peter by the hand and lifted him out of the water.

"You of little faith," Jesus said to Peter, "why did you doubt?"

When Jesus and Peter got back into the boat, the winds died down and the waves were calm.

The Disciples Get a Show

Matthew 17:1-13

Jesus was the Son of God. In fact, he was God himself. It was hard for the disciples to understand who Jesus really was. So one day Jesus decided to show them. He took Peter and James and James's brother, John, up to a high mountain.

What happened there?

Jesus began to shine right in front of them. His face looked like the sun, and his clothes became as white as light.

Only the four of them were there on the mountain?

No. Moses and Elijah were there too. And they were talking to Jesus.

Who were Moses and Elijah?

Moses was the one God used to lead the people of Israel out of Egypt and to cross the Red Sea. And Elijah was the prophet who defeated the prophets of Baal. God took Elijah up to Heaven in a chariot.

What did the disciples think when they saw Moses and Elijah?

They were thrilled. "It is good for us to be here," Peter told Jesus. "Let's build a tent for each of you."

So did Peter build the tents?

No. Just then a bright cloud came down over the mountain and covered them up.

And then what happened?

The disciples heard a voice. "This is my Son, whom I love," the voice said. "With him I am well pleased. Listen to him!"

What did the disciples do then?

They knew it was God speaking to them. The disciples were terrified. They went down on their knees and worshipped.

Did Jesus say anything to them?

Yes. He touched them on their shoulders. "Get up," he said. "Don't be afraid."

Did they get up?

Yes. When they opened their eyes and looked up, only Jesus was there.

What happened then?

Jesus and the disciples walked down off the mountain. Jesus told the disciples, "Don't tell anyone what you have seen until I've been raised from the dead."

Learning to Forgive

Matthew 18:21-35

Do you forgive people when they do something wrong? Or do you try to punish them or get back at them? God always forgives. And he wants us to forgive others too.

One day Peter asked Jesus how many times he had to forgive people.

What did Jesus say?

Jesus told Peter there was no set number of times to forgive. Peter had to continue forgiving people. Then Jesus told a story.

What was the story about?

The story was about a king. A lot of people owed the king money.

What did the king do?

One day a man who owed the king a lot of money was brought to him. The king said the man and his family should be sold as slaves to pay him what he owed.

What did the man say?

He fell down on his knees and begged the king. "Be patient with me, and I will pay you back," he said.

What did the king say?

The king felt sorry for the man. He told the man he didn't have to pay back what he owed him, and he let him go.

What did the man do?

The man went out and looked for another man who owed him some money. He shook the man and said, "Pay back what you owe me!"

What did the man say?

The man got down on his knees and begged the man, "Be patient with me, and I will pay you."

Was he patient with him?

No. He threw him into prison until he could pay him back.

Did the king find out about that?

Yes. His servants heard about it and told him.

What did the king do?

He called the man back in and reminded him that he forgave him because he asked him. But he should have forgiven the other man in the same way.

So what did the king do to him?

He sent him to prison.

Jesus told this story to teach us how important it is for us to forgive people. After all, God forgave us, didn't he? It wouldn't be very nice for us to be forgiven by God and then to not forgive others, would it?

Jesus Helps a Blind Man

John 9:1-41

Jesus and his disciples were going to worship God in the temple one day. When they arrived, they saw a man sitting at the gates to the temple. He had been blind ever since he was born. He always sat at the gates to the temple, asking people for money.

The disciples asked Jesus, "Who sinned, this man or his parents, that he was born blind?"

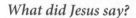

Why did the disciples ask that?

In Bible times many people believed that when someone was sick, it was because God was punishing them for disobeying him. Since this man had been born blind, perhaps God was punishing his parents.

What did Jesus say?

"Neither this man nor his parents sinned," Jesus said. "He was born blind so that people would praise God."

What did that mean?

This man had been born blind so that he could be at the temple and Jesus could heal him, and God would be given the glory for the healing.

Is that what Jesus did?

Yes. He spit on the ground and made mud. Then Jesus spread the mud on the man's eyes. He told him, "Go, wash in the pool."

Could the man see?

Yes! He came back from the pool able to see. People saw him walking around and wondered whether he was the same man who had always been blind. He said, "I am the man."

What did the Pharisees, the Jewish leaders, say?

They were upset because Jesus had made the mud and healed the man's eyes on the Sabbath (a special day dedicated to God, like Sunday is to us today). So they called the man in to their meeting so they could talk to him.

What did the man tell them?

He told them what happened, how Jesus made mud and rubbed it on his eyes, and that after he washed in the pool, he could see. The Jews asked the man what he thought about Jesus, and he said he believed Jesus was from God.

So what did the Jewish leaders do then?

They didn't believe that the man really had been blind. They wanted to talk to his parents.

What did his parents say?

They told the Pharisees that he was their son and that he was born blind. But they told them to ask the man himself if they wanted to know how he was healed and how he could now see.

So did the leaders ask the man again?

Yes. They wanted him to say that Jesus was not from God. But the man said they could decide that themselves. "One thing I do know," he told them. "Once I was blind, and now I can see."

He told them of his experience with Jesus. That's the same thing we all can do—tell people what Jesus has done for us.

What did the Pharisees do then?

They kicked the man out of the temple. Jesus heard what happened and went to find him. He asked the man if he believed in him. The man said yes, and he began to follow Jesus.

The Woman at the Well

John 4:1-42

Jesus and his disciples were traveling. They walked from Jerusalem in Judea all the way up to Galilee. It took several days to make the trip of about 90 miles. Jesus and his disciples had to walk everywhere they went, so it took a lot longer to travel than it does now.

Jesus chose to walk through Samaria. Samaria was located between Judea and Galilee. Sometimes Jews would cross over the Jordan River and walk an extra day so they didn't have to walk through Samaria.

Why wouldn't they walk through Samaria if that was the shortest route?

It goes back to when the nation of Israel was defeated by Assyria. Some of the people stayed in the country and married the Assyrians. The Jews never accepted their children, the Samaritans, because they weren't fully Jewish.

Did Jesus and his disciples stop to rest along the way?

Yes, they stopped at Sychar as they were walking through Samaria. Jesus rested at Jacob's well. Jacob was the grandson of Abraham, the father of the nation of Israel. The disciples left Jesus there and went into town to buy food.

Was Jesus alone at the well?

At first he was alone, but then a Samaritan woman came to get some water from the well. Jesus asked her to get him a drink.

She was surprised Jesus was even talking to her. "You are a Jew and I am a Samaritan woman. How can you ask me for a drink?" she said to Jesus. Remember, Jews and Samaritans didn't like each other. And men didn't talk to women like her either.

Did she know who Jesus was?

No. "If you knew who it is that asks you for a drink," Jesus said to her, "you would have asked him, and he would have given you living water. Those who drink of the living water will never thirst again."

Did the woman know what that meant?

No, she asked Jesus how he could get her this living water if he didn't even have a jar. She wanted to have the living water so she didn't have to keep coming to the well every day.

Did Jesus explain what he meant?

Not right then. He told her to go get her husband. She said she didn't have a husband.

What did Jesus say?

"You're right," Jesus told her. "You have had five husbands. And the man you are living with now isn't your husband."

What did she say to that?

She told Jesus that he must be a prophet and that someday the Messiah was coming and he would explain everything.

Did Jesus tell her then who he was?

Yes. "I who speak to you am he," Jesus said.

What did the woman do then?

She left her waterpot at the well and went back home to tell all her friends about Jesus.

Did they believe her?

The woman urged her friends to come and see Jesus for themselves. Many believed in him because of what she had told them about Jesus and what he said to them. That's our job too. To bring our friends to Jesus. We don't need to convince them to follow Jesus. Jesus will convince them himself. We just need to introduce our friends to Jesus.

Jesus Raises Lazarus

John 11:1-44

Jesus and Lazarus were best friends. In fact, Mary and Martha, Lazarus's two sisters, were close friends with Jesus too. Do you have good friends like that?

One day, Lazarus became very sick. Mary and Martha sent a message to Jesus.

What did the message say?

They told Jesus, "Your good friend Lazarus is very sick."

What did Jesus do?

He went to see Lazarus. But Jesus waited two days before he went.

Was Lazarus still alive?

No. Lazarus had died and they had wrapped up his body and buried it in a tomb.

Who happened when Jesus arrived there?

Mary, Lazarus's sister, ran out to meet Jesus. She told him that if he had been there, he could have healed Lazarus and Lazarus wouldn't have died.

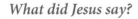

What did Jesus say?

He asked Mary to show him where they had buried Lazarus. She took Jesus out to the tomb.

What did Jesus do next?

He told the men to move the stone away from the front of the tomb.

Did they do that?

Yes. Martha, Lazarus's other sister, said that it would smell awful. Lazarus's dead body had been in there for several days. But Jesus insisted.

Then what did Jesus say?

He prayed to God. He prayed that God's name would be glorified and that people would know how powerful God is.

Did Jesus say anything else?

Jesus turned to the tomb and said, "Lazarus! Come forth!"

What happened?

Lazarus came out of the tomb. He could hardly walk because he was all wrapped up.

What did Jesus do?

He told the men to unwrap Lazarus and let him go. They were thrilled, and many began to follow Jesus after that.

Jesus Is Anointed with Oil

John 12:1-11

Jesus was the Son of God. He came to Earth to die on a cross to save us from our sins. Not everyone knew that.

Jesus always went to Jerusalem for the Passover meal. But one year's Passover was special. That year Jesus would be put to death on the cross. Before the Passover, Jesus went to the house of some friends for supper.

Whose house did Jesus go to?

He went to have supper with Lazarus and his sisters, Mary and Martha, at their house in Bethany.

Who cooked the meal?

Martha prepared and served the meal.

Was Lazarus there?

Yes. Lazarus ate the meal with Jesus.

Were other people there too?

Yes. They wanted to see Jesus and Lazarus. Earlier Lazarus had died, and Jesus raised him from the dead. So many of the Jews wanted to see both Jesus and Lazarus.

What was Mary, Martha's sister, doing?

Mary opened up a jar of very expensive perfume.

What did Mary do with the perfume?

She poured it on Jesus' feet and then got on her knees and wiped his feet with her hair.

What did people say?

One of the disciples, Judas, was upset. He said that the perfume should have been sold and the money given to the poor. That perfume was very expensive—it was worth about the amount of money someone would earn in a year.

What did Jesus say?

He said to leave Mary alone. "You will always have the poor among you," Jesus said, "but you will not always have me."

Mary did the right thing. She spent all her time with Jesus. A good lesson for us all!

Jesus Enters Jerusalem

Mark 11:1-11

It was the Sunday before Passover, the main festival for the Jews. Many, many people came to Jerusalem for Passover. It was a very special time.

Why was Passover so special?

During Passover, the Jews remembered how God saved them from slavery in Egypt. The Lord's Supper was started as part of the Passover meal.

Did Jesus and his disciples attend Passover?

Yes. Every year. Jesus would always go to Jerusalem to attend Passover and then begin traveling again.

One year, Jesus went to Jerusalem on Sunday, almost a full week before Passover began. It would be a special day.

What happened on that Sunday to make it so special?

First, Jesus told two of his disciples to go into a neighboring town. He told them they would find a colt tied up there.

What were they supposed to do when they found the colt?

Jesus told them to untie the colt and bring it back to him.

They couldn't just take the colt, could they? Wouldn't someone stop them?

Some people standing around there saw what the disciples were doing.

"What are you doing, untying that colt?" they said. Jesus had told them just what to say if someone asked that question, "The Lord needs it and will send it back here shortly," they told them. And the people let them go.

So what did Jesus do when the disciples brought the colt back?

After the disciples laid their cloaks on the colt, Jesus sat on it. Then, riding the colt, he entered the city of Jerusalem with his disciples.

Did anyone notice?

Yes, people ran over and cheered when they saw Jesus.

Did people do anything?

They grabbed palm branches and laid those on the ground in Jesus' path. They also laid their cloaks down on the ground.

Did they say anything?

They shouted, "Hosanna! Blessed is he who comes in the name of the Lord."

"Blessed is the coming kingdom of our father David!"

"Hosanna in the highest!"

Was everyone cheering for Jesus?

No, some of the leaders of the Jews didn't like what was happening. They told Jesus to tell the people to be quiet. But Jesus told them that if the people didn't yell out, the rocks would cheer.

What did Jesus mean by that?

Jesus was the Son of God. Many, many years before Zechariah had prophesied this event, he told the people to cheer for joy because their King was coming, riding on a colt. So, if the people were quiet, even the rocks would cry out.

The Final Meal

John 13:1-30

Jesus and his disciples never missed the Passover meal. This time was more special, though. The disciples got together in the upper room to eat the Passover meal together.

Why was this Passover meal so special?

Jesus told his disciples that he would not eat the Passover meal with them again until he returned to set up his kingdom. This would be his last Passover meal with them on Earth.

What happened during this meal?

Jesus got up from the table. He took off his outer cloak and wrapped a towel around Himself.

Then what did he do?

Jesus began to wash the disciples' feet. In Bible days, people walked everywhere on dirty roads. They wore only sandals, so their feet became very dirty. It was normally the servant's job to wash the guests' feet.

What did the disciples do?

Peter wouldn't let Jesus wash his feet. He thought he should be the one washing Jesus' feet. But Jesus told Peter to let him do it.

So did Peter let Jesus wash his feet?

Yes. Peter told Jesus to wash him all! But Jesus said that he only needed to wash his feet.

What did Jesus say then?

He told the disciples that they were to do the same thing, to serve each one another just as Jesus served them.

Then Jesus told them that one of the disciples was going to betray him.

What did the disciples say to that?

Peter turned to John and said, "Ask Jesus who it is."

Is that what you would have done if you found out one of your friends was telling on you?

What did John do?

He asked Jesus, of course.

And what did Jesus say?

"It is the person who takes the bread," answered Jesus, then he gave a piece of bread to Judas. He said to Judas, "What you do, do quickly."

Did the disciples know why Jesus said that to Judas?

No. Judas was the disciples' treasurer, so they thought it had something to do with money. Judas left right away.

Did Judas betray Jesus?

Yes, later, in the garden of Gethsemane, Judas was the one who led the soldiers to Jesus so they could arrest him privately without any people around.

Jesus Came to Die

John 18:1–19:16

Everyone dies. But Jesus came to Earth to die. Without Jesus' act of dying on the cross, there would be nothing for us as Christians to tell others. Without Jesus' dying on the cross, he would not be our Savior. When Jesus died on the cross, he made it possible for us to go to Heaven with him. He made it possible for God to forgive us.

It was now time for Jesus to die. He knew that, even though his disciples did not. One night Jesus was praying in his special place and soldiers came to arrest him.

How did the soldiers know where Jesus was?

Judas, one of Jesus' disciples, was with them. He had led the soldiers to Jesus.

Did any of the disciples try to stop the soldiers from arresting Jesus?

Yes. Peter grabbed his sword and cut off the ear of one of the high priest's servants.

What did Jesus do?

Jesus told Peter to stop. Then he healed the servant's ear.

Did the soldiers arrest Jesus then?

Yes. There was no reason for Jesus to fight them. This was part of God's plan for him.

Where did they take Jesus?

They took Jesus to the high priest, Caiaphas.

What did he do?

Caiaphas started asking Jesus questions about his teaching. But Jesus told him that he taught out in the open. If he wanted to know anything about Jesus' teaching, Caiaphas could ask the people who heard Jesus speaking.

What did the high priest say about that?

The high priest sent Jesus to Pontius Pilate, the Roman governor who was in charge of everything involving the Jews.

What did the Roman governor say?

Pilate talked to Jesus. He didn't find him guilty of anything. He told the Jews that he usually released one of the prisoners this time of year. He asked them, "Do you want me to let Jesus go or Barabbas?"

What did the Jews say?

They told Pilate to free Barabbas.

Did Pilate free Barabbas?

Yes. Then he had Jesus whipped and gave him over to the Jews.

What did the Jews do to Jesus?

They made Jesus carry a cross, and the Romans put him to death. Jesus had never done anything wrong, but he died because of our sins. Jesus died in our place.

Jesus Is Alive

John 20:1-31

The Jews and the Romans thought they were through with Jesus. Jesus had died, and they thought that was the end of him. But they were so wrong.

Jesus died on Friday. First thing Sunday morning, Mary Magdalene went down to the tomb to prepare Jesus' body for burial.

Why did Mary Magdalene wait until Sunday morning to prepare Jesus' body?

Jesus died late Friday afternoon. The Sabbath, the Jewish holy day each week, begins Friday evening and ends Saturday evening. So Sunday morning was the first time Mary could get to the tomb to prepare Jesus' body.

Was Mary able to get into the tomb?

Yes. When she got to the tomb, the stone in front had been rolled away. Mary thought the body of Jesus had been taken somewhere else. After all, Jesus had been placed in a borrowed tomb.

What did Mary do?

She went to get Peter and John, two of Jesus' disciples. "They have taken away the Lord, and I don't know where they put him," she said.

Peter and John ran as fast as they could to the tomb.

What did they see when they got there?

They saw the white linen sheets Jesus had been wrapped in lying in the tomb. But Peter and John still didn't understand what Jesus said about being raised from the dead.

So what did they do?

Peter and John went back home, but Mary Magdalene was very upset. She just stood outside the tomb and cried.

Was anyone else there?

Yes. Mary looked inside the tomb and there were two angels sitting there.

"Why are you crying?" they asked.

What did Mary say?

"They have taken my Lord away, and I don't know where they have put him," Mary answered.

Just then Mary saw a man standing outside the tomb. She turned to ask him about Jesus' body too.

What did he say?

Mary did not know it was Jesus. So Jesus turned to her and said, "Mary." That's all she needed to hear. She said, "Teacher!" Now she knew Jesus was alive.

Jesus told her to tell the disciples that she had seen him and that he was alive.

Did the disciples believe Mary?

Yes. She went to see the disciples and told them that she had seen Jesus. She told them that soon Jesus would be going back to Heaven.

Did the disciples see Jesus?

Yes. On Sunday evening they were in the upper room. The doors were locked because they wanted to be safe from the Jews. Suddenly, Jesus appeared to them.

They were thrilled! Jesus told them that soon they would be receiving the Holy Spirit, but first he must return to Heaven.

Did Jesus return to Heaven?

Yes, but first he spent many wonderful days teaching the disciples everything they needed to know. Then Jesus went up to Heaven to be with God. And he is there today, at God's right hand, watching over us and helping us every day.

Jesus Helps Peter Fish

John 21:1-22

Peter loved to fish. He had been a fisherman for many years. When Jesus met Peter, he told Peter he would make him a "fisher of men." After everything that had happened to Peter and the other disciples when Jesus died and rose from the dead, Peter needed to relax.

What did Peter do?

One night Peter told the other disciples that he was going fishing.

What did they say?

The other disciples told Peter they would go fishing with him. So they all took the boat out and went fishing.

How long were they out fishing?

They fished all night long. They didn't catch anything.

So what happened?

In the morning, a man on the shore saw them fishing. He asked them if they had caught anything, and they told him no.

He told them if they would try fishing on the other side of the boat, they would catch some fish.

What did the disciples do?

They did what the man said and put their nets on the other side of the boat.

And what happened?

The disciples caught a lot of fish! In fact, they caught 153 *large* fish. They began to tow the netful of fish to the shore where the man was waiting for them.

Just then John, one of the disciples, recognized the man on the shore.

Who was it?

Jesus! John turned to Peter and said, "It's the Lord!"

What did Peter do?

Peter became very excited. He put his outer garment back on and jumped out of the boat. He was so excited to see Jesus.

What about the other disciples?

They were bringing the boat to shore, dragging the net filled with the fish.

What was Jesus doing on the shore?

Jesus already had a fire going for the fish. He told the disciples to give him some of the fish to cook on the fire.

Did they have breakfast?

Yes. Jesus cooked the fish and gave the disciples fish and bread to eat. This was the third time the disciples had been with Jesus since he was raised from the dead. They learned again that if they followed the Lord and did what he said, they would be okay.

The Holy Spirit Comes

Acts 2:1-41

The disciples were sad. Jesus, their Lord and God's Son, had returned to Heaven. But Jesus told them not to worry. He told the disciples to return to Jerusalem and wait.

What was going to happen in Jerusalem?

Jesus told them that the promised Holy Spirit was going to be sent to them. They were all together in the upper room of a building in the city. They prayed and waited. And waited.

Did something finally happen?

Yes. Suddenly, a strong wind came from Heaven. The entire building shook, and the wind filled the room in which the disciples were sitting.

Was that the Holy Spirit?

Yes. The Bible describes him as a mighty wind. Along with the wind were tongues of fire. The tongues separated and rested on each person's head.

Did that change the disciples at all?

Yes. Not only did it give them great power but they began to speak in other languages.

Did they know other languages?

No, they knew only their own language. But the Holy Spirit gave them this special ability to speak in languages they did not know.

Did anyone hear them?

Yes. It was at the time of a special Jewish feast in Jerusalem, the Festival of the Harvest. There were people there from all over the world who spoke different languages.

What did the people think?

They were amazed. The people didn't understand how the disciples could be speaking in all these different languages. "What does this mean?" they kept wondering.

Did anyone know the answer?

No. Some of the people were making fun of the disciples, though. "They've had too much to drink," they said.

What did the disciples say?

Peter stood up and got everyone's attention.

"These men are not drunk," he said, "It's only nine o'clock in the morning!"

Then he explained that the Holy Spirit had come and that this was predicted by the prophet Joel many years ago. Peter then went on to tell them that Jesus was God's Son, and they had put him to death on the cross.

Peter always found a way to tell people about Jesus. Just as we all should do.

How did the people respond to that?

They were shocked and upset and worried.

"What should we do?" they asked Peter and the disciples.

"Repent and be baptized," Peter told them.

So did they repent?

Yes. In fact, 3,000 people were baptized right then and joined the church! They knew they had done wrong and wanted to get right with God. The only way to do that, even today, is to accept Jesus as your Savior.

Philip Chases A Chariot

Acts 8:26-40

Philip was an evangelist. His job was to tell people about Jesus. There was a road south of Jerusalem that went out into the desert. One day God told Philip to go out on that road.

Did Philip know why he was supposed to go out on a road in the middle of the desert?

No. Philip just obeyed God. Sometimes we don't know why God tells us to do certain things. We just need to be ready to do what he says.

What happened when Philip got to the road?

Philip met an Ethopian man who was on his way home from Jerusalem. This man was an important official in Ethiopia. He was in charge of all the queen's money and possessions.

What did he do in Jerusalem?

Jerusalem was a special place. The temple of God was in Jerusalem. It was the place everyone went to pray and worship God. The Ethiopian man had just worshipped God there.

What was Philip told do?

The Holy Spirit told Philip to catch up to the Ethopian man's chariot. When he got near the chariot, Philip heard the man reading Isaiah 53:7.

Did Philip say anything to the man?

Yes. Philip asked the Ethiopian man if he understood what he was reading. The Ethiopian man said, "How can I unless someone explains it to me?"

What did Philip say?

Philip told him that Isaiah was writing about Jesus. He then told the man the good news of the gospel.

Just then the chariot passed some water and the Ethiopian asked Philip, "Why shouldn't I be baptized?"

What did Philip say?

"If you believe, you may be baptized," Philip told the man.

"I believe," the man told Philip. So Philip and the Ethiopian got out of the chariot and Philip baptized the man. The man was saved, all because Philip obeyed God's instructions.

You never know where God may want you to go to tell people about Jesus. You just need to listen and obey.

Saul's Conversion

Acts 9:1-19

Do you have any enemies? Are there any bullies at your school, kids who like to be mean and scare everyone? Right after Jesus returned to heaven, when the church was just getting started, the Christians were scared of a bully named Saul. Saul made a promise to himself to do everything he could to destroy the church.

Why did Saul hate the church so much?

Saul was a very strong Jew. He attended the best Jewish schools and studied the Scriptures hard. He thought the Christians were wrong to tell people that Jesus was the Son of God. He wanted to get them to stop.

So what did Saul do?

Saul went to see the high priest, the leader of the Jews. He wanted to go to Damascus, a nearby city. Saul asked the high priest for permission to arrest Christians there and bring them back to Jerusalem and put them in jail.

Did the high priest give him permission?

Yes, he did. So Saul got a group together and traveled to Damascus to arrest the Christians who were there.

What happened when Saul got to Damascus?

Actually, Saul and his group never made it. When the group got close to Damascus, a bright light flashed down from heaven onto Saul.

What did Saul do?

Saul fell down to the ground. He heard a voice from heaven. The voice said, "Saul, Saul, why are you persecuting Me?"

Who was it?

That's exactly what Saul wanted to know. "Who are You, Lord?" Saul asked.

"I am Jesus, whom you are persecuting," the voice answered. "Now get up and go into the city, and you will be told what to do next."

What did the other people in the group do?

They were stunned. They all heard Jesus' voice, but they didn't see him. When Saul got up, he was blind.

So how did he get into the city?

The men in the group helped him. They lifted him up and led him by the hand.

What happened once Saul reached the city?

He was there for three days. Saul still couldn't see. He didn't eat or drink either.

Didid God contact Saul again?

There was a man named Ananias who believed in Jesus. God told Ananias in a vision to go see Saul and to help him see again.

Did Ananias go to visit Saul?

He didn't want to go at first. Ananias was scared of Saul because Saul had been so mean to the Christians. But God told Ananias that Saul would be serving him now and Ananias shouldn't be afraid.

Saul was able to see again as soon as Ananias touched and told him how God was going to use him to tell everyone about Jesus. Saul was now a member of God's team!

Saul Preaches About Jesus

Acts 9:19-30

After Saul became part of God's team he spent several days with the disciples in Damascus. He studied the Bible. Saul learned a lot about Jesus.

One day Saul attended the synagogue, the special place Jews went to worship and learn about God.

What did Saul do in the synagogue?

He told people about Jesus.

Did the people recognize Saul?

They did and they were amazed. "Isn't this the person who wanted to kill all the Christians?" they said. They didn't understand why he was now telling people Jesus was God's Son.

Did Saul stop talking about Jesus?

No. Saul knew the Scriptures so well that he could prove to everyone that Jesus was the Son of God and that they should believe in him. Saul did everything he could to please God and to convince the people of Damascus to follow Jesus.

What did the people do?

They weren't happy. They wanted to kill Saul.

How were they going to kill him?

The Jews guarded the city gates of Damascus so they would know when Saul tried to leave the city.

Did they find Saul?

No, Saul knew about their plan. So, late at night, Saul's friends lowered him in a basket through an opening in the wall, and he went to Jerusalem.

What did Saul do in Jerusalem?

He went to see the disciples there, but the disciples wouldn't let him in to see them. They knew Saul as the person who wanted to destroy the Christians, and they didn't trust him.

So what did Saul do?

He talked to Barnabas. Barnabas took Saul to the disciples. He told them everything that had happened to Saul and how he had told everyone in Damascus about Jesus.

So did the disciples believe Saul then?

Yes. Saul stayed with them for a while in Jerusalem.

What did Saul do in Jerusalem?

Saul did the same thing that he had done in Damascus. He told everyone about Jesus. Saul ended up arguing with some Jews from Greece. It became such a big argument that the Jews wanted to kill Saul.

Then what happened?

The disciples took Saul up to Caesarea. There he was able to take a boat to Tarsus. Tarsus was Saul's hometown, and he would be safe there.

Peter Heals Aeneas and Dorcas

Acts 9:32-42

Peter was a special disciple of Jesus. He loved Jesus very much and was determined to serve him and help others as Jesus had done. Jesus told Peter that he was the rock upon which Jesus was going to build his church. One of the good things Jesus did was to help people. Peter tried to help people too. One day when Peter was traveling, he came to the town of Lydda.

What did Peter do in Lydda?

Peter told people about Jesus. There he met a man named Aeneas, who was a paralytic. Aeneas hadn't been able to walk for eight years. He was lying on a mat.

Did Peter help Aeneas?

Yes. "Aeneas," Peter said to him, "Jesus Christ heals you. Arise and pick up your mat."

Right away Aeneas picked up his mat and walked away.

What did everyone think of that?

People were amazed when they saw Aeneas walking around Lydda. They all believed in God and began to follow Jesus too.

Was Peter able to help anyone else?

Right next to Lydda was the town of Joppa. A woman by the name of Dorcas lived there. Everyone loved Dorcas because she was always helping people.

What happened to Dorcas?

One day Dorcas became very sick. Soon she died. Her body was placed on a table in an upper room of her house.

Did Dorcas's friends know Peter was nearby?

They heard he was in Lydda, yes. A couple of men went to see him and ask him to come to Joppa.

Did Peter go with them?

Yes. Peter went to Joppa with the men. When they arrived at Joppa, the men took Peter to see Dorcas's body. Many people came to talk to Peter and tell him how much they had loved Dorcas. They showed Peter all the nice clothes Dorcas had made for them.

What did Peter do?

Peter asked everyone to leave the room. Then he prayed for Dorcas.

Did Peter help her?

Yes. Peter looked at her dead body and said, "Dorcas, sit up!"

Did Dorcas sit up?

Yes. She opened her eyes and saw Peter. Then she sat up.

Did the other people know she was alive?

Peter called them back into the room. They were thrilled! Soon everyone in Joppa heard that Dorcas was alive again. They accepted Jesus as their Savior too.

Peter Learns That God Loves Everyone

Acts 11:1-18

Do you love everyone? Do you think God loves everyone? Did Jesus die for everyone, or just for people like you? What about people in other parts of the world? Or people who are a lot different from you?

Peter thought Jesus died only for people like him—the Jews. After all, Jesus was a Jew, and Peter and all the disciples were Jews. Peter thought God loved only the Jews.

But then something happened to change Peter's mind.

What happened?

Peter was in the city of Joppa. As Peter was praying, he saw a vision from God.

What was in the vision?

There was a large sheet being let down from heaven.

Was anything on the sheet?

Yes. Live animals were on the sheet—animals, birds, and snakes.

Then what happened?

God told Peter to kill the animals and eat.

But Peter told God, "I will never eat anything that is unclean." The Jews have many rules about what they should and should not eat.

What did God say?

"Don't call anything unclean that God has called clean," God told Peter. This happened three more times. Then the sheet and all the animals went back up to heaven.

What did that all mean?

That's what Peter was trying to figure out. But just then three men came to the house and asked for Peter. These men were not Jewish. They were different from Peter.

What did the men want?

They told Peter that an angel of God had told them to come get him. That Peter could tell them how to be saved. This was hard for Peter because Peter thought only the Jews could be saved.

So what did Peter do?

He went with the men to a house.

What happened when Peter got there?

Peter told them about Jesus. He explained how they needed to accept him and stop disobeying God.

Did the people at the house believe Peter?

Yes. They accepted Jesus as their Savior. And Peter saw something else too.

What was that?

Peter saw them receive the Holy Spirit from God. After they accepted Jesus to be their Savior, the Holy Spirit gave them the ability to speak in different languages, and they had power from God to do special things for him, just as all the disciples did.

Peter was convinced. God loved everyone and wanted everyone to be saved. So, the next time you see someone who doesn't seem to look or act like a Christian, think of Peter.

Peter Escapes Prison

Acts 12:1-19

God always answers prayer. Sometimes God answers prayer right away, and sometimes he answers prayer later. And then there are times when God answers prayer before we even ask him. Because, you see, God knows what we're going to ask even before we pray. That's what happened to the people in the early church one night long ago when they prayed.

Who were they praying for?

Peter, the apostle. He had been arrested and was in jail. King Herod was attacking the early Christians and even had one of the leaders, James, put to death. He then arrested Peter and chained him to two guards and locked him up in prison.

How did Peter get out of prison?

Peter was asleep one night, chained to two guards as usual. Suddenly a bright light shone from the sky directly into the prison cell. An angel of the Lord came, woke Peter up, and told him to put on his cloak and sandals and follow him. The chains just fell off Peter.

Did Peter follow the angel?

Remember, Peter was sound asleep when the angel woke him. He thought he was seeing a vision or dreaming. He did not realize this was really happening to him. But he did what the angel said.

When did Peter wake up?

Peter and the angel walked out of the prison, and when they got to the gate that led into the city, the gate opened by itself. Suddenly the angel left, and Peter was standing there all alone. He then realized that God had sent his angel to rescue him.

Where did Peter go?

Peter went to Mary's house. Mary was the mother of John Mark. John Mark is the apostle who wrote the Gospel of Mark. People were there praying for Peter.

God knew the need before they even asked him, and he had already solved the problem. He does that with us too. He knows our needs and helps us.

What did Peter do?

He knocked on the gate outside
Mary's home. One of the servants,
Rhoda, came to the gate and saw
Peter.

Did she let him in?

No. She went back inside to tell the
people who were praying that Peter was
right outside.

What did they say?

They didn't believe her. "You're out of your
mind," they told her. They probably thought
she was seeing things or dreaming. They
were praying for Peter, and there he was, right
outside the house. God doesn't answer prayer
that fast, does he? Or, does he?

So what did Peter do?

He kept knocking at the gate.

Did they finally open the gate and let him in?

Yes, when Peter continued to knock, the people came out and finally let him in. They were very shocked to see him there and had a lot of questions for him.

What did Peter say?

Peter held up his hand to get them to be quiet and explained everything that had happened to him. How God sent his angel to rescue him from prison. Peter then went on to another home to tell people what had happened and to praise God for taking care of him.

A Great Earthquake

Acts 16:16-40

God takes care of his people. And that includes you. One night Paul and his good friend Silas were arrested. But God took care of them. Even in jail.

Why were Paul and Silas arrested?

Paul and Silas told people about Jesus. They met a slave girl who possessed evil power that allowed her to predict the future. Her owners made a lot of money using her as a fortune-teller. But when Paul healed her and made her well, she could no longer make money for her owners. They became so upset they had Paul and Silas arrested.

What happened to Paul and Silas?

The leaders of the city tore the shirts off Paul and Silas and had them beaten. Rather than plain whips, whips made with pieces of metal were used. Paul and Silas were bleeding afterward.

Did the leaders take them to a doctor?

No. The city officials took Paul and Silas direct-ly to prison and told the jailer to guard them and make sure they did not escape.

How did he do that?

The jailer took Paul and Silas to the in-ner jail, the most secure jail cell he had. He locked their legs and arms in stocks to be sure they did not escape.

Did that keep them in jail?

Yes. But Paul and Silas were not scared. They knew God would protect them. In fact, late at night, around midnight, Paul and Silas were having their own worship service. They were praying and singing worship songs. All the other prisoners were listening to them.

Did the guard tell them to stop?

No, he was asleep.

Then what happened?

Suddenly, there was an earthquake. The earthquake was so big it shook the entire building. All the doors in the jail sprang open, and the prisoners' chains fell off.

Did they all escape?

That's what the guard thoughthad happened. He woke up from his sleep and saw the doors open and thought he had lost all the prisoners.

The guard pulled out his sword and was going to kill himself. Just then Paul yelled out to him, "Don't do that; we are all here!"

Why would the guard want to kill himself?

Because the guard's job was to make sure none of the prisoners escaped. If he lost even one prisoner, especially if he was asleep, he would be tortured and killed.

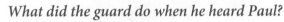

What did the guard do when he heard Paul?

He took some lights and ran inside the prison where Paul and Silas were and made sure they were all there. The guard took Paul and Silas out of their jail cell and said to them, "Please, tell me, what must I do to be saved?"

What did Paul say then?

Paul answered very simply, "Believe in the Lord Jesus Christ and you will be saved."

So that night Paul explained the gospel to the guard and his family. They were all saved.

Paul's Nephew Helps

Acts 23:1-35

The apostle Paul had been arrested. The Jews did not like Paul. Paul told people about Jesus. He told people that Jesus was the Son of God. The Jews did not like that. They wanted Paul to stop telling people about Jesus.

Did they tell Paul to stop telling people about Jesus?

Yes! They brought Paul in before the Sanhedrin, the leading group of the Jews. It would be like someone in our day going before the Supreme Court of the United States.

What happened?

Paul told them that he was on trial because he believed in the resurrection of the dead.

Did that make the Jews happy?

No, actually, that made them angrier. Half of the Jews believed people could be resurrected from the dead, and the other half did not believe a person could be raised from the dead.

So what happened?

The two groups of men started yelling at each one another. They argued so much that the soldiers were afraid Paul would be killed. They removed Paul from the room for his safety.

Was Paul worried?

Wouldn't you be? But then God appeared to him at night and told him not to worry. "Take courage," God told Paul.

Was Paul safe then?

No, a group of more than 40 Jews made a promise that they would not eat anything until Paul was dead. They went to the Sanhedrin, the leaders of the Jews, and told them to tell the soldiers that they wanted to talk to Paul again and ask him some more questions.

Then they would be waiting to attack and kill Paul when they brought him to meet with the Sanhedrin.

Did their plan work?

It probably would have if Paul's nephew had not overheard them talking.

What did he do?

He went right to Paul and told him about it.

What did Paul say?

Paul called a soldier over and asked him to take his nephew to the commander. The commander took Paul's nephew by the hand and asked him, "What is it you want to tell me?" Paul's nephew told him exactly what the Jews were planning.

Did the commander help him?

Yes. He arranged for 200 soldiers, 70 horsemen, and 200 spearmen to sneak Paul out at nine o'clock at night. Not only did he take Paul to a place where he would be safe, there were more than 600 Roman soldiers to protect him. Not much a group of 40 men could do!

Once again, God took care of Paul and kept him safe, just as he does for us all.